Sins of the Saints

Sins of the Saints

by

G. D. Rosenthal

Morehouse-Gorham Co.
New York
1958

First Edition published in 1938
by Harper & Brothers

Revised Edition published in 1958
by Morehouse-Gorham Co.

Library of Congress Catalog Card No. 58-13713

BV
4625
, R67
1958

Printed in the United States of America

Preface

I WAS once told the story of a young priest who had many of the gifts that go to the making of a preacher. He was eloquent and earnest, and took great trouble over the preparation of his sermons, but he was miserably conscious that his preaching had no effect on the lives of those who listened to him, and that he was failing to win souls for Christ. One day, feeling quite desperate, he went to another priest who was himself an effective preacher, and said to him: "What is wrong with my preaching? For all my efforts I don't seem able to influence people at all." "Your trouble, my dear fellow," said the other, "is that you have mistaken your audience. You are preaching not to the man in the pew but to the man in the moon." "Whatever do you mean?" said the young priest. "I mean," said the older man, "that the questions you discuss are not human questions; the problems with which you deal are not human problems; the language you speak is not human language. Give up preparing your sermons on the assumption that the man in the moon will be the only person present, and talk to the man in the pew in his own language about his difficulties, and his temptations, and his shortcomings, and his opportunities, and you will soon find a response to your message."

This book is written for the man in the pew. The word *saint* in its title, as in the title of an earlier volume of mine, *The Saint in the Street,* is used not as connoting exceptional spiritual gifts, or deep mystical experience, but, in the sense in which St. Paul uses it, as a description of ordinary Christian folk who are making an honest effort in their daily lives to obey the teaching of Jesus Christ and to follow His example. We should most of us agree that we are not very successful in that attempt, and I am persuaded that one of the chief reasons for our failure is our tendency to look at sin through the eyes of the world and not through the eyes of Christ. So long as we think of sin as murder, or fornication, or adultery, or theft, or deliberate lying, or drunkenness, so long will our penitence be unreal, for these are, commonly, not our sins, but when we look at sin through the eyes of Christ, and see that for Him it was a more perilous state for a man to be self-satisfied, or money-loving, or censorious, or uncharitable, we have to readjust our standards.

I make no claim to originality for what is written here. Indeed, if there were anything new in this book it would not be true, for to a Christian the principles of conduct are absolute and constant; it is only their application that is relative and changing. These chapters are based not only on my own experience as a parish priest for more than thirty years, but on the reading of a great many books; and I owe so much to the thoughts of others, that only a general acknowledgment of my indebtedness is possible. As in my other books, I have made many quotations from the poets, for I have always been convinced that the melody and imagery of poetry are of the highest value both in arousing attention, and in impressing truth on the memory.

No one could write on such a subject without feeling the force of the saying: "Physician, heal thyself." Let me repeat, then, what I have already implied in the dedication, that I recognize no difference between the pulpit and the pew in this matter, and associate myself entirely with those for whom this book is written. Indeed, the writing of it has brought home to me, most vividly, the grave responsibility that rests upon those who, like myself, are called to teach others when they need to be instructed themselves.

G. D. ROSENTHAL

"Therefore let us also, seeing we are compassed about with so great a cloud of witnesses, lay aside every weight, and the sin which is admired of many, and let us run with patience the race that is set before us, looking unto Jesus the author and perfecter of our faith, who for the joy that was set before Him endured the cross, despising the shame, and hath sat down at the right hand of the throne of God."

Hebrews xii. 1, 2 (R.V. Marginal rendering).

Contents

1

The Sin That Is Admired of Many

THE PICTURE set before us in the twelfth chapter of the Epistle to the Hebrews suggests the Roman amphitheater, with its thousands of spectators sitting on crowded benches, tier above tier, to watch the conflict. "Wherefore," says the author, "seeing we also are compassed about with so great a cloud of witnesses, let us lay aside every weight, and the sin which doth so easily beset us, and let us run with patience the race that is set before us, looking unto Jesus." (The Authorized Version.)

Most people when they read this passage think that "the sin that doth so easily beset us" means the besetting sin, the particular sin which each person finds himself confronted with most frequently and persistently. (Most lists of self-examination questions mention this sin especially.) If we put that question to ourselves we are almost sure to think about some bad habit of ours, such as fault-finding, uncharitable talk, slothfulness, carelessness about our prayers, or a tendency to lose our tempers over trifles. That is not what the author of this Epistle means here: he is not thinking about self-indulgence, or vindictiveness, impatience or bad temper; he has in mind something altogether different.

The Greek word which our Authorized Version translates "doth so easily beset us," is not found anywhere else in the New Testament or in classical literature. Quite literally it means "surrounded by those who much admire it," or as the margin of the Revised Version has it, "admired of many." The figure has a close connection with the cloud of witnesses just mentioned. As the saints surround us and encourage us when we do right, so the world surrounds us and applauds us when we do wrong. In other words, "the sin that is admired of many" is the popular and respectable sin.

There is an old Latin proverb to the same effect which may be rendered, "We perish by permitted things." It is just here, for reasons that we shall consider presently, that the greatest danger to our souls lies, not in the sins whose wickedness everybody acknowledges, but in the sins which most men do not regard as sins at all. It is unlikely, though not of course impossible, that any readers of this book will lose their souls by murder, embezzlement, adultery, forgery, perjury, or by any of the notorious sins which are condemned and denounced by the ordinary standards of decent society. No, we are much more likely to perish, if we perish at all, by "permitted things," by "the sin that is admired of many," which is openly acknowledged without shame and talked about freely and without restraint. Wherefore, says the writer in effect, seeing that the saints are watching us as we play our part in the drama of life, let us accept *their* standards, and not the standards of the world which is also watching us. Let us lay aside as the saints did not only the notorious sins which all respectable people acknowledge to be wrong, but the popular sins, the applauded sins which the world actually regards as virtues—if it bothers to think of them at all.

The sins which this book deals with are nearly all of this kind. You will find that scarcely one of them is not surrounded by a crowd of admirers, either inside the Church or out of it. We could commit them quite openly and freely without losing our position in society or our standing with our friends. These sins find their origin in the acceptance of the world's standards of conduct instead of the standards of Christ, and may be classified under the comprehensive term, "worldliness."

What exactly do we mean by "worldliness"? It is very important to be clear about this, for the word "world" has various meanings in the New Testament, and many good people have gone dangerously astray by failing to distinguish between them. Sometimes it means the whole universe in its order and beauty—so St. Paul says, "For the invisible things of Him since the creation of the world are clearly seen, being perceived through the things that are made." Sometimes it means this earth, as when the tempter showed our Lord "all the kingdoms of the world, and the glory of them." Or it may mean the inhabitants of the world, as when we are told that "God so loved the world." Lastly, and most often, it means those who are living apart from God, unbelievers, faithless Christians, and especially the great pagan organization of Rome. This is the world we are told we must not love, and from which we are to keep ourselves unspotted. This is the world whose pomps and vanities we renounced at our Baptism, its pomps and vanities, along with all covetous desires of the same.

The failure to understand the difference between the world we must love and the world we must not love has resulted in a corrupt form of "other-worldliness" which has so often been characteristic of religious people, leading them to make a false division of life into sacred and secular, to be preoccupied with the things of eternity at the expense of the things of time, and to forget that the ideal of Christendom is to establish the throne of Christ not merely in some separated, fenced-off corner of life which they dignify with the name of religion, but in all its provinces and departments; in literature, in art, in science, in trade, in politics, in international relations. From this kind of "other worldliness" has arisen the deplorable complacency with which so many Christian people still regard preventable social and economic evils, and the concentration on personal piety to the exclusion of any attempt to solve the moral problems involved in social relations. Such an interpretation of other-worldliness is a caricature both of the teaching of the New Testament and of the historic Faith of Christendom.

Worldliness, let me insist again, is the acceptance of popular standards of life and conduct instead of the standards of Christ; it is dependence on public opinion as opposed to the will of God. We are not worldly because we love the ordered harmony and beauty of nature; or because we delight in social life; or because we realize the duties and responsibilities of our earthly citizenship; or because we are keen about our work and want to make a success of it; or because we are intensely interested in the success of the human conquest over nature, the advance of scientific knowledge, and the improvement of human conditions of life and work. In all these senses a Christian should love the world and not despise it. If, however, we measure life by the world's yardstick; if we think, as the world thinks, that money and social position, power and popularity are the things best worth striving for; if we trim our consciences so that we may stand well with those around us; if we measure people not by what they really are in point of character but by their position or income; if we are ready to trade the "Well done" of God for the good opinion of men; if we prefer the seen to the unseen, the material to the spiritual, the temporal to the eternal; then, however outwardly religious we may be, we are worldly men and women, and the prince of this world reigns in our hearts. This is the worldliness against which our Lord and His Apostles warn us and which we renounce at our Baptism: this is what the writer of the Epistle to the Hebrews means by "the sin that is admired of many."

Worldliness, strangely enough, is the peculiar temptation of religious people. The attractiveness of worldliness lies in its "respectability"—and in the fact that we are intensely proud of being respectable. It is quite respectable, for instance, to love money or to speak uncharitably. These are sins which are "admired of many," and in general we are not ashamed of them. But how deeply ashamed we would be if it were known that we drank too much, were guilty of adultery, or were convicted of theft! We have our own standards, true enough, and we who flout them do so at our own peril. The trouble is that our standards are *worldly* standards. (We simply cannot afford to commit notorious sins; public opinion is too strong for us!) And so it is that the whole power of the devil tempts us to the admired, the applauded sins, the sins which the world regards as respectable.

These are precisely the sins which our Saviour condemned most severely. It has often been pointed out that the moral judgments of our Lord are sometimes unexpected. He is severe where we would be soft, and soft where we would be severe. The sins that stirred Him most were not the sins that the world condemns; they were the sins that the world admires. To the woman taken in adultery He said: "Neither do I condemn thee; go and sin no more." Of the harlot who washed His feet with her tears, He said: "Her sins which are many are forgiven, for she loved much." But to the religious Scribes and Pharisees who were universally respected, who were the religious people of their time, and who were guilty of the popular and accepted sins of pride, exclusiveness, love of money, self-satisfaction and the like, He said: "Ye serpents, ye generation of vipers, how can ye escape the damnation of hell? The harlots and publicans go into the Kingdom of God before you." All through the Gospel story it is the same. His sternest judgments are always kept not for the sins we Churchfolk dare not commit lest our reputations suffer, but for the sins which are "admired of many," the sins for which the world applauds us, or for which at least it thinks no less of us if we commit them every day.

How are we to overcome worldliness? Let St. John tell us: "This is the victory that overcometh the world, even our faith." The writer of the Epistle to the Hebrews gives us precisely the same teaching when, after bidding us lay aside the sin which is admired of many, he continues in the next sentence: "And let us run with patience the race that is set before us, looking unto Jesus." As the saints of the Old Testament lived by faith in the Christ Who was to come, so we must live by faith in the Christ Who has come, Whose earthly life was the perfect type and pattern of human goodness, and Who came down from Heaven not only to teach us and to die for us, but to leave us an example that we should follow in His steps. The imitation of Christ has been the perpetual source of saintly effort in the Church; generation follows generation "looking unto Jesus." And we in our turn, if we aim to form the Christian character, must take Christ as our standard. To act as He would have acted in our particular circumstances, with our particular temptations and opportunities, to think as He would have thought, to speak as He would have spoken, so that little by little "Christ is formed in us" and we are transformed into His likeness—that is the inspiring ideal which our religion sets before us.

Wherefore, seeing that we are in the heroic succession of the blessed saints of God who compass us on every side, let us lay aside the sin which is admired of many, and run with patience the race that is set before us, looking unto Jesus. He did not hang in agony upon the Cross of shame that you and I might be respectable; the standards of the world, the code of man are enough to make us that. He poured out His heart's blood to make us His own, that we might give ourselves to Him in complete surrender, dedicating ourselves, body, mind and soul to His service, and striving day by day to follow the steps of His most holy life. His voice comes down to us today across the gulf of ages. He sees in us His own image, the stuff of which His heroes and saints are made. He shames us out of our worldliness, rouses us out of our self-satisfaction. He charms us by the worldly hopes which He shatters and wins us by the witchery of Heaven. He takes us in His holy and venerable hands, blesses and breaks us. He bids us to be in the world and yet not of it; to use the world as not abusing it; to obey its rightful claims and yet defy its claim of sovereignty over us. He says to us in that sweet but imperative voice of His: "Take up thy Cross and follow Me."

2

The Controversial Spirit

THE late Bishop Trollope of Korea once told me that when the American Church began mission work in that country great difficulty was found in translating its title "Protestant Episcopal Church" into Korean. Help was sought from a learned native scholar who finally produced a phrase which, when rendered back into English, was found to mean *The Society of Contradicting Overseers.*

An unkind critic might say that this is an appropriate title for the Universal Church, and we must admit that there is much in its history to support such a contention: from its earliest days the Church has been torn by dissension. When we contemplate the intolerance, the jealousy, the malice, the spite which have been displayed in religious controversy, the vituperation used in connection with it, the violence and persecution that have accompanied it, we may be disposed to marvel that Christianity has survived at all. It has done so because it is so much greater than the controversies which have disgraced it. The storm passes, the ocean with its fathomless depths remain.

Religious controversy is a sorry business and the Anglican Communion has a particularly bad record with regard to it. Its members, more perhaps than those of any other religious body, have been and still are split into parties which engage in constant bickering and strife. Now religious dissension is to a certain extent inevitable and it becomes a duty, at times, to defend the Faith even when we know that will involve controversy. This is particularly true among Anglicans since we are engaged in the dangerous, the delicate, but, as I believe, the most hopeful experiment of attempting to make a synthesis between authority and freedom; but the controversy between different parties in the Anglican Communion frequently passes beyond all reasonable bounds, is often pursued in a most unChristian spirit and does grievous harm to the whole cause of true religion. God alone knows the whole extent of the damage done to the credit of Christianity by inter-Christian controversy but some of its disastrous consequences are open to our observation.

To begin with, outside the limits of ecclesiastical circles, our continual dissensions have created in the mind of the average man an infinite weariness and disgust. It is not that he objects to controversy in itself: he thoroughly enjoys a heated argument, and when it is a question of politics or economics or some other secular affair he is as ready to wield his cudgel as the next man; but he has an inward conviction that perpetual controversy is entirely out of place between those who claim that brotherly love is the first principle of their religion. He will tell you, if he is frank, that he thinks we are all to blame because we fail so grievously in sweet reasonableness and Christian charity. He does not understand the merits of our disputes or realize the importance of the principles that underlie our differences. What he feels is that we are presenting to the world a very sorry exhibition of Christianity, which he interprets far more in terms of conduct than of creed. Our interminable quarrels have strengthened his conviction that no religious truth has any real authority at all. The dislike of dogmatism in religion seems to him to be amply justified. He therefore relapses into complete indifference or turns on the radio or television on a Sunday to find escape from ecclesiastical discord in the uncontroversial ethics of the air waves.

Secondly, controversy always tends to distort perspective and to upset what St. Paul calls the proportion of the Faith. It gives such prominence to some particular doctrine or practice that everything else is forced into the background or crowded out of the picture altogether. The idea of the Church, as a living organism, its evangelistic mission, its strong and vigorous moral discipline, its sacramental interpretation of the beauty and dignity of life, its passion for social righteousness, its enthusiasm for the weak, the suffering, and the oppressed, its sense of fellowship and of the solidarity of humanity in Christ—these are the things that ought to stand out so strikingly in the foreground of the picture that they would be recognized immediately as the essentials of the Christian religion. They are the "weightier matter" and they tend to be forgotten or ignored while we quarrel with one another about far less important things.

The distortion of Christian perspectives is magnified immensely by the wide publicity given to our controversies in secular newspapers. The reporter, in his professional capacity, is interested in religion only so far as it can provide him with a story. Controversy makes a story, while worship and devotion do not. The public is always interested in a fight, be it a dog-fight or a prize-fight, or that most envenomed of all conflicts, a clergy-fight. When the Church is good copy it is so (as a rule) for the worst of reasons and with the worst possible results.

But what of the *religious* press? We are likely to blame our Church papers for their controversial spirit and, like the rest of us, they are certainly open to criticism for the provocative and uncharitable language in which they sometimes indulge. Let us be fair. A religious newspaper is like any other paper in this respect: its first duty is to get itself read. If it fails to do that it lacks the principle of life and dies. If it is to get itself read it must deal with matters that are of interest to its readers, and its editor gets a very clear indication of what his public wants from his mail-bag. The worst feature of our religious papers is provided not by the editors but by ourselves. It is not the features or the editorial comments but the correspondence columns that are most blameworthy for bitterness of invective, for intolerance and party spirit and for most unseemly wrangling between those who ought to be prepared to make every possible allowance for one another. Not content with washing our dirty linen within the parish we send bundles of it to the Church papers, to be laundered in the presence of the whole Anglican Communion. So far, at least as Churchpeople are concerned, the writing of controversial letters to the religious press is one of the sins that are "admired of many."

Once more and perhaps above all, controversy tends to interfere with devotion and to damage the sensitivity of the soul. It breeds self-satisfaction, unfairness, uncharitableness, intolerance and much else that disturbs communion with God. It is for this reason that controversy ought always to be rigidly excluded from the pulpit except when the plain proclamation of the Faith may lead to it. The Faith comes first and must be preached even in the face of dissent, but the preacher, be he bishop or priest, if he is to be of real help to souls, must be positive and constructive. His true function is to bless, not to curse; to teach, not to criticize; to build up, not to tear down; to affirm, not to deny. Avoidable controversy degrades the pulpit; it harms the priest (or bishop), his congregation, and his cause; and it suggests that those who indulge in it are woefully deficient in intellectual and spiritual resources. (Nothing is so easy as destruction.)

As was said earlier we cannot always avoid controversy. Even when we want to, our belligerent neighbor will not let us; and at times we find it impossible to escape from it without a surrender of principle. After all it was worthwhile for Athanasius to convulse the Church for a diphthong since that diphthong involved the truth of the Incarnation, however destructive the Arian controversy may have appeared at the time. The fundamental doctrines of the Christian Faith are not matters for compromise or concession: they are an inheritance which we must preserve unimpaired even at a cost of dissension and division so that we may hand them on in their integrity to the generations that follow us. Therefore, bitterly as we may regret the results of controversy, we cannot get rid of it altogether, even if it does alienate public opinion, distort perspective and hinder devotion. The practical problem for us is how we are to shun and avoid not so much controversy itself, but rather the controversial *spirit;* how we are to behave in an atmosphere of dissension so as to rob controversy of its worst evils. As has been well said: "He who would use the weapons of controversy aright, whether in attack or defense, must look to it that he wears the right equipment, or he will find himself injured by the very force of the weapons he was trying to wield." When we Christians are compelled to engage in controversy we are in special need of the grace of

God, for we have to make an exceptional call on our store of virtue.

First we need humility. Truculence and self-assertion are very bad arguments for Christianity, and the only effect of paying our opponents back in their own coin is to depreciate the value of the Gospel currency. We are apt to pay our own particular orthodoxy the quite indefensible compliment of assuming that there is no truth at all outside of it. We are much more likely to be persuasive and convincing when we are humble and tolerant than when we are cocksure and aggressive.

Secondly we need charity. Needless to say this much-abused term does not commit us to a vapid indifference or a false courtesy that is willing to tamper with the truth. Charity forbids utterly the use of the world's weapons—scorn, contempt, bitterness, misrepresentation, unfair argument, the imputation of unworthy motives, as being both contrary to our Christian profession and completely powerless to effect that for which they are called into action.

Thirdly we need pity. After all it is a solemn and serious thing to be called to draw the sword in the cause of God. The Crusaders are not the only people who, starting in a holy war, turned it into an armed raid. There are some verses of John Henry Newman much of whose life was spent in unavoidable controversy, which are as searching as they are pertinent:

Thou to wax fierce
In the cause of the Lord,

To threat and to pierce
With the heavenly sword!
Anger and zeal
And the joy of the brave,
Who bade thee to feel,
Sin's slave?

The altar's pure flame
Consumes as it soars,
Faith meetly may blame
For it serves and adores.
Thou warnest and smitest,
Yet Christ must atone
For a soul that thou slightest—
Thine own.

It will help us to moderate our ardor in controversy
if we remember that most of the things about which
Christians have disputed most fiercely usually have been
matters of passing moment. History indeed has taught
us no more important lesson on this subject than that
of the permanence of the Church and the evanescence
of its controversies. No one cares today about the controversies that fill St. Paul's Epistles about circumcision
and the Jewish Law in its relation to Christianity, and
so on: they are read today not because of their long-
defunct disputations, but because of the positive truths
they contain. Gnosticism and Docetism, Montanism,
Pelagianism, Arminianism, and many others that might
be named simply do not exist for the modern Christian
in their ancient form, yet at one time they were *the*

religious questions of the hour, and some of them created divisions that lasted for centuries. The same thing is true of many of the controversies that convulsed the Church at the Reformation, questions about Justification, Election, Final Perseverance and theories of the Atonement and the like. It is true that behind the controversies there were often principles that still live and are of value, but the particular form in which they roused fierce dissension have completely passed away and have long since been forgotten by most Christians. So too, will it be with most of the controversies that disturb the peace of the Church today. Time, the great arbiter, will solve them in such fashion that succeeding generations will be hard put to it to know what all the quarrelling was about.

It comes to this: the only controversies that are really permanent in their effects are the controversies that take place far from the world's arena, in the secret places of the soul. The conflict between good and evil, between love and hate, between duty and pleasure, between old habit and newly-won conviction: these are the decisive battles of a man's life which he has to fight out in silence, without publicity, and in the presence of God; these are the true religious controversies in which every disciple of Christ must take sides. We need all our strength in fighting the evil within us. How foolish to squander our spiritual resources in fighting one another!

3

Bad Temper

BAD temper may be defined as the controversial spirit in private life, and it bears to anger much the same kind of relation as the controversial spirit does to controversy. As we saw in the last chapter controversy cannot always be avoided—it is the controversial spirit that is never justifiable. Similarly, while anger may be a virtue, bad temper is always a sin. There were occasions when our Lord was angry: He looked upon hypocrites with anger being grieved for the hardness of their hearts, He was angry with the money-changers who profaned His Father's House, sometimes He was angry with His disciples, but it is impossible even to imagine Him being ill-tempered. In His example we see the working out in practice of the apostolic precept: "Be ye angry, and sin not."

Anger, indeed, so far from being intrinsically evil, is an instinctive emotion, part of our natural equipment for protecting ourselves and those we love from injustice and ill-treatment. Primitive man needed it far more than we do for he had constantly to be on the defensive against dangers from which we are guarded by the protection of civilized society. While we have inherited the emotion in its full strength, we have far less reason for its exercise with the result that we possess an enormous surplus capacity for anger—and this we tend to pervert into ill-temper, instead of directing it into legitimate channels. Many of our sins have a similar origin. They are simply savage qualities, sometimes even savage virtues in their old age. They spring from the deeply-rooted conservatism of the instinctive life, its tendency to go on in the changed circumstances, acting in the same old way. Thus when we yield to implacability, or resentment, or the desire for revenge, or sulkiness or spite, or any of the many forms in which ill-temper displays itself, we are relapsing into a lower stage of creation when instinct acted without the control of either reason or grace.

Few people [said Miss Evelyn Underhill] go through life without knowing what it is to feel a sudden, even murderous impulse to destroy the obstacle in their path; or to seize at all costs that which they desire. Our ancestors called these uprushes the solicitations of the devil seeking to destroy the Christian soul; and regarded them with justice as an opportunity of testing our spiritual strength. It is true that every man has within him such a tempting spirit; but its characters can better be studied in the Zoological Gardens than in the convolutions of a theological hell.

Anger, then, is not sinful in itself; it is sinful only

when it escapes from the control of reason and con-science, and degenerates into ill-temper. Righteous anger, restrained but not quenched, has in it a wonder-ful power for good. It rouses our indignation against wrong and stirs us up to resist evil. If we are trying to be like Christ there are times when we shall certainly be angry. To quote Bishop Butler:

The indignation raised by cruelty and injustice, and the desire of having it punished which persons unscorned would feel, is by no means malice. No, it is resentment against vice and wickedness, it is one of the common bonds by which society is held together, a fellow-feeling which each individual has in behalf of the whole species as well as of himself. And it does not appear that this, generally speaking, is at all too high amongst mankind.

Whether or not it be true, as Bishop Butler suggests, that there is not enough moral indignation in the world, it is certainly true that there is far too much bad temper. We must also admit, if we are honest, that there is quite as much bad temper inside the Church as outside it. This is indeed one of the com-monest vices of the virtuous. Probably the reason for this is that people have very little conscience with re-gard to it. They think they are born to it, that it is no fault of theirs, that it is their misfortune rather than their fault. This is particularly noticeable about those who yield to passionate outbursts of anger: they are likely to regard these tempests of ungoverned emotion as something deserving of congratulation. "I know I have a quick temper, but it is soon over, and I never sulk." How often we hear people say that as if it were something very much to their credit! They will excuse some cruel word or unkind action on the ground that they were angry. "I was in a temper at the time," they say, "I didn't really mean it." Every priest who has tried to help people to repent knows how difficult it is to make them realize that bad temper is a sin. I do not know of any other sin, with the possible exception of depression, about which so many and such varied excuses are made. We are not disposed to palliate it in other people but we are very slow indeed to recognize it as sinful in ourselves. We plead jaded nerves or a sluggish liver or depressing circumstances, or claim as fact that those around us are so provoking, or, above all, blame our temperament for which we have no more right to be blamed than for the color of our hair. Indeed the color of the hair is popularly supposed to have something to do with it. "I know I've got a hasty temper," said a girl to me once, "but then I'm Irish and have got red hair so what can you expect?"

There is just enough truth in all this to make it specious. The control of temper is much more easy for some people than for others because their temperament is more easy-going and phlegmatic, or because their health is better, or their conditions of life more harmonious or less trying on the nerves. Such well-balanced folk do not feel the pressure of adverse circumstances so much as the rest of us do. Their self-poised nature tends to make them accept provocations passively. On the other hand there are those who have inherited an ill-balanced temperament and are upset by every trivial irritation. Geniuses are a case in point. They are interesting to read about but, as a rule, difficult to live with. I remember some old verses which I read as a boy and which put this tersely. It is an inventor's wife who is speaking:

> It's easy to talk of the patience of Job;
> Job had nothing to try him.
> If he'd only been married to 'Bijah Brown
> Folks wouldn't have dared come nigh him!

Similarly we always think of Xanthippe as a shrew, and our sympathy is all for her husband, Socrates. I have no doubt the lady had a case; her husband must have been intensely irritating at times. Geniuses lack poise, they are impulsive and ill-balanced, they are "without method, plus a good deal of madness." The world would be poorer without its geniuses, but it would be far more peaceful.

Few of us are geniuses or can claim their excuse for failure in self-control. Our lack of balance is not due to the over-development of some faculty or talent which makes a positive contribution to science or literature or art. It is simply the result of our obstinate refusal to admit that bad temper is a sin, and our consequent unwillingness to make the necessary effort to conquer it. The control of temper can be achieved; it is far more often a grace than a gift. It can be acquired more effectively than it may be inherited. In the lives of the saints we find many examples of men and women naturally impetuous and violent who by resolute purpose and humble dependence on God's grace realized self-restraint as a natural habit of the soul. St. Teresa, to take but one instance, said that the devil sometimes sent her so offensive a spirit of bad temper that she could eat people up. In her case, and in the case of others like her, self-control was all the more impressive because of the reserved strength of bridled passion held in leash behind it. What she did in the face of a vehement and excitable disposition we too can do—if we will. It is no good our saying we cannot control our temper; we *must* control it if we are to be worthy of the Name we profess. A Christian who gives rein to his passion, who is constantly sulky, fretful, or impatient dishonors his Lord, fails in charity to his neighbor, and brings shame and scandal on his religion. It must not be so, and it need not be so, if only we realize that bad temper is a grievous sin.

It will help us to do this if we reflect on the unhappiness it causes. Bad-tempered people are a thorough nuisance. Wherever you come in contact with them, be it on a committee, a Church organization, in a club, workshop or office, they sow the seeds of dissension, make work difficult, create an atmosphere of unpleasantness and discord, and ruin healthy and happy social intercourse. Wherever he goes, whatever company he frequents, a quarrelsome man finds something at which to take offense, some cause of complaint and indignation. He passes his life in injuring and receiving injury, in making others unhappy and in being made wretched himself. Thus he is always violating charity which, as St. Paul reminds us, "is not easily provoked." Is everyone really in league against him? Is he really worse treated than anyone else? Has he really more to put up with than other people? Not a bit of it! His trouble is that he has never learned to control his temper: the result is that provocations of little importance to others become serious matters with him and call forth the full torrent of his indignation. We know how degrading ill-temper is in others. We know how it makes them say and do the cruel and wicked things they would never dream of saying and doing in their sober senses. How is it that we cannot see that the effects of bad temper are precisely the same in ourselves?

Add to all this that bad temper hurts most those whom we love most. Out in the world we have to mind our manners more or less: we cannot say or do exactly what we like without suffering for it in pocket or in credit; but at home it is different—there we can take the lid off, let the reins loose; and how often we do, saying bitter things which are not easily forgotten, inflicting wounds which do not easily heal, for which occasional gifts and bursts of good nature do not atone!

Sulkiness, fretful irritability, the nursing of grievances, the habit of nagging and complaining, the determination to have the last word at all costs—these are among the greatest enemies of home life, for they make love wither at its roots. The old Hebrew proverb is the record of a bitter and all too common experience: "It is better to dwell in the wilderness than with an angry and contentious woman; it is better to dwell in the corner of the housetop than with a brawling woman in a wide house." (The proverb is just as true if we substitute the word "man" for the word "woman.") As life advances love deepens or it fades: it deepens if every trial or difficulty is taken as an opportunity for mutual help and sympathy; it fades if every passing anxiety or worry is made the occasion for a display of temper.

The best safeguard against ill-temper is silence. Here more than in anything else it is true that "silence is golden." St. James puts the control of the tongue and the control of the temper together when he says: "Let every man be slow to speak, slow to wrath." In this, as in all else, our Lord is the supreme example. His silences were always impressive and significant but never more so than during His Passion. Through those heavy hours, cross-woven with hate and spite and jealousy, He fulfilled Isaiah's prophecy: "As a sheep before his shearers is dumb, so he openeth not his mouth." Not once was He embroiled in the strife that went on all about Him; no provocation disturbed His inward peace or stung Him into making a sharp retort. If He had refused to answer His accusers at all, His silence would still have taught us how much can be endured. But He did reply to some of their charges, yet His silence, when He chose to keep it (as when standing before Herod, "He answered him never a word,") reveals the fineness of His temper and the quality of His endurance. No word was ever wrung from Him. When He spoke He did so out of the quiet of infinite patience, out of the light of unclouded counsel, out of the leisure of unhurried decision.

We may learn from the silent Christ that there are falsehoods too false to be worth a denial, charges too baseless to be worth refuting, insults too cruel and vindictive to be worthy of a reply. There is a battle that is won with a sheathed sword; there is an argument of endurance that words can only weaken; there is debt of silence that in the name of his manhood and of his spiritual dignity a man sometimes owes to his own soul. When we are tempted to yield to ill-temper there is no prayer that will help us more than this: "Set a watch, O Lord, before my mouth. Keep thou the door of my lips."

4

Unwillingness to Forgive

I THINK most of my readers will agree with me
when I say that the forgiveness of injuries is one of
the most difficult of Christian duties. It is easy enough
to write about, but it is very hard indeed to put into
practice. No doubt this is partly because the world, on
whose "good opinion" we are so apt to rely, regards
meekness (of which the readiness to forgive is the most
characteristic expression) as a cowardly and poor-
spirited thing; but the chief reason is that it goes
against the grain of human nature and is directly
opposed to our self-regarding instincts. Forgiveness is
not natural to the human heart; it is an exotic growth
in an unfriendly soil. If someone cuts us in the street
after being perfectly friendly elsewhere, how spontane-
ously the demon of resentment rises in our hearts! If
we hear that a friend whom we have trusted has
spoken evil of us, how quickly our love turns to hate!
If a man under the cover of friendship induces us to
put money in a business which he knows to be unsafe

and we lose savings that we can ill spare, how hard it is when the crash comes to resist the desire for revenge! Or, it may be, there is someone for whom we have made great sacrifices and on whose gratitude we have a substantial claim. The time comes when we in our turn need his help, when a little kindness or sympathy from him would mean a great deal to us, and we who have relied upon it find that it is withheld. How keenly and quickly our sense of injury rankles, how difficult we find it to forgive or forget! At such times the law of "an eye for an eye, and a tooth for a tooth" appeals to us with wellnigh irresistible attractiveness. In the Church, as in the world, an unforgiving spirit is most certainly to be numbered amongst the sins that are "admired of many."

We need, then, a powerful motive to enable us to resist the pressure of public opinion and our own self-regarding instincts: we need to be *willing* to forgive those who have wronged us. That motive the Christian religion supplies. St. Paul, in the Epistle to the Ephesi-ans, expresses it in words that are at once most simple and most persuasive when he says: "Be ye kind to one another, tenderhearted, forgiving one another, as God, for Christ's sake, has forgiven you."

For the sake of Christ! It would be impossible for a Christian to have a more compelling motive than that. It quickens the heart of every true disciple. It contains the principle of all life for God. For Christ's sake His blessed Mother was obedient to the angel's message and clasped to her heart the piercing sword of agony which was inseparable from the privilege of divine Maternity. For Christ's sake the disciples left all to follow Him. For Christ's sake the martyrs endured the scourge and rack and flame. For Christ's sake the saints struggled through doubt, temptation, and sin to holiness. If we have ever had grace to conquer sin, it has been given us for Christ's sake. If in the voluminous records of our lives there is written down any virtue and any praise, it was something we did for Christ's sake, and for Christ's sake it has been accepted. So too in the matter of forgiving injuries. What we find impossible to do for any lower motive we may gain strength and grace to do for Christ's sake.

"Forgiving one another for Christ's sake" means, in the first place, forgiving one another in obedience to His express and reiterated *command*. He is more exacting about this than about any other duty; He insists upon it as something that is absolutely necessary for our salvation. "I say unto you, love your enemies, do good to them that hate you, pray for them that despitefully use you." "With what judgment ye judge, ye shall be judged, and with what measure ye mete, it shall be measured to you again." So, too, in answer to St. Peter's question: "Lord, how often shall my brother sin against me, and I forgive him; til seven times?" He makes the startling reply, "I say not unto thee until seven times but until seventy times seven," that is to say, again and again, indefinitely. Then He proceeds to drive home the duty with the parable of the Unmerciful Servant whose own forgiveness was cancelled because he was unforgiving, and ends with the solemn warning: "So likewise shall my heavenly Father do also unto you, if ye from your hearts forgive not everyone his brother their trespasses." In teaching us to pray ("Forgive us our trespasses as we forgive those who trespass against us"), our Lord keeps ever before us the reminder that we can hope for forgiveness only if we are forgiving in our turn. How can we pray the Lord's prayer if we are cherishing revengeful and vindictive feelings? What is it but to say: "Lord, I hate my enemy; do Thou in like manner hate me. I refuse to forgive him; take not away mine offenses. I would be revenged on him; take Thou vengeance on me. I will not speak to him; be Thou deaf to my call." When we pray "Forgive us as we ourselves forgive," we affirm that we are at least trying to fulfill the condition which alone justifies our asking for forgiveness. We may try imperfectly but we must try. Before we can make the petition for ourselves we must be doing our very best to let the spirit of charity and forgiveness take possession of our hearts.

"Forgiving one another for Christ's sake" means also forgiving one another in imitation of His example. Those of us who are called to give religious teaching to others must confess with shame how often and how lamentably we fail to put our precepts into practice. It is not so with our Master. His teaching is part of Himself, for God *is* love. No depths of depravity or degradation ever separated those who sought mercy and pardon from Him during His earthly life. Publicans and outcasts, harlots and other open and notorious sinners had only to seek forgiveness to obtain it. He was equally forgiving to those whose sins were directed personally against Himself. He freely forgave the disciples who deserted Him, St. Peter who denied Him, St. Paul who persecuted Him. When He was pierced by the hands of wicked men, He blotted their sin out of His Father's thought in that great prayer of pardoning love: "Father, forgive them for they know not what they do." And now that He reigns in glory at His Father's side, His forgiveness is still freely offered to each one of us. He is "the same, yesterday, today and for ever." "His compassions fail not; they are new every morning." Long He has borne with us, and countless as have been our offenses, yet as often as we repent He is willing to wash us in His cleansing blood and to forgive us until seventy times seven. That is how Christ deals with us, and that is how we ought to deal with one another. For our lifework is to imitate His character, and by our baptism we profess to follow the example of our Saviour Christ and to be made like unto Him.

Once more, "forgiving one another for Christ's sake" means forgiving one another out of gratitude for what He has done for us. If we would find strength for forgiveness, let us lift up our eyes to the Cross and behold the Man of Sorrows nailed there for our sakes. He

Who hangs on the Tree of shame is the God-made-Man Who willingly endured that awful death that we might be forgiven. From the height of that Cross He calls to us: "This is what I have done for your sake. Will you not forgive one another for My sake?" Here is the most powerful motive of all. This is to forgive not merely from fear of punishment or from a sense of duty but royally, out of love and gratitude to Him Who poured out His soul unto death for us men and for our salvation.

On a Good Friday morning a thousand years ago, a young nobleman named John Gualbert was seeking the murderer of his only brother. He found him unarmed and drew his sword, but from the lips of his defenceless foe came the appeal that his enemy might spare him, and that the Lord Jesus Who died on that day would save his soul. The thought of Christ hanging on the Cross giving His life for mankind touched the young knight's heart. "I cannot refuse," he said, "anything that is asked me for the sake of Him Who died on this day. I not only spare your life, I give you my friendship. Pray for me that God may pardon my sin, and be thou a brother to me in the place of the brother I have lost." It was the turning point in the two lives. Together they founded the Monastery of Vallambrosa and there retired from the world. What a commentary on the apostolic exhortation: "Be ye kind to one another, tenderhearted, forgiving one another, as God, for Christ's sake, has forgiven you."

So much for the *motive* of Christian forgiveness, but what about its measure? We are to forgive as God has forgiven us. The word "as" means not only because, but in like manner. What then are the characteristics of the divine forgiveness?

First, divine forgiveness is *righteous;* that is to say it is bestowed upon us only when we repent. This follows from its very nature. Forgiveness is a gift, and like any other gift it can be offered to all but it can be received only by those who are willing to accept it. What another person forces me to take is not a gift but an imposition. No man's sins are forgiven until he himself by his own free act has claimed and accepted forgiveness. There is always forgiveness in the heart of God, but forgiveness cannot be made effective unless it is claimed and taken. The essential condition which enables us to receive and appropriate the divine forgiveness is repentance.

The same is true with our forgiveness of one another. We must always show a forgiving spirit, but we have no right to bestow forgiveness where there is no repentance, we *cannot bestow* it. We may *offer* it, as God always offers it to us; but, in the one case as in the other, it depends on the wrongdoer—whether it *can be received*. Our Lord's teaching on this point is precise and definite: "If thy brother trespass against thee, rebuke him, and if he repent, forgive. And if he trespasses against thee seven times a day, and if he turns to thee seven times a day saying I repent, thou shalt forgive him." The Christian religion does not lay on us the impossible duty of indiscriminate and unconditional forgiveness. Malice, vindictiveness, the desire for revenge find no place in the heart of God, and they must find no place in the heart of a Christian. But forgiveness in its positive sense, the blotting out of the memory of an injury, the treating of it as if it had never been, the receiving back of the offender into the circle of intimate friendship—all this is impossible without repentance. And if it were possible it would not be righteous. To treat wrongdoing lightly is to spare an individual at the cost of impairing the moral tone of the whole community. If that tone is to be kept healthy and vigorous there must be the expression both in words and deeds of an intense disgust for selfishness, meanness, and falsehood, not only when they injure others but when they cause injury to ourselves.

Assuming that he who has injured us is sorry for having done so (as in nine cases out of ten he is, though very possibly he has not the courage to say so in so many words), then our forgiveness of him ought to be real. Such is God's forgiveness of us. It is full, free, and magnanimous. He retains no trace of anger; He forgets our sin and casts it behind Him. He trusts us again with all His former confidence; He never upbraids. So our Lord pictures the divine forgiveness in the pearl of parables: "When he was yet a great way off his father saw him, and had compassion, and ran, and fell on his neck and kissed him."

Is our forgiveness like that? You will sometimes hear people say: "I will forgive, but I cannot forget." Or, "I will forgive him, but we can never be the same again." Such statements are mere words; they mean less than nothing at all. Or people will say, "I am willing to receive explanations." If what seemed a wrong can be explained it requires no forgiveness. Where would we be if God's mercy went no further than this—a willingness to receive explanations? There are those who make the very form of their forgiveness the instrument of revenge: they will forgive with an ostentatious display of magnanimity, a parade of generosity, a loud denial of any angry or hostile feelings—all as alien as possible from the true Christian temper. (There are some people whose revenge is less bitter and more tolerable than their forgiveness.) Though there is a formal reconciliation, unkind feelings and resentment go on, it may be, for years—and often about very little things: a statement is misinterpreted, a word is exaggerated, an action is misunderstood, and then it is: "I will never forgive him." "I will never speak to her again." Sometimes when the parish priest has been the offender it is: "I will never enter the church again"—not merely that particular church but any church. I remember once a member of my own congregation left for no apparent reason; months afterward I discovered what had made him stop coming to Church: I had passed him in the street without noticing him! Need I say it was no intentional discourtesy? Do not, then, take offense where it is not intended, and do not exaggerate it even when it is intended. This has been somewhat of a digression but not an unimportant one. Let me return to the main point with the reminder that our forgiveness must be like God's forgiveness, first righteous, and secondly, real.

Thirdly, it must be *repeated*. We must be ready to forgive one another as God forgives us, again and again and again. We think a great deal of it if anyone commits a fault against us a second and a third time; but we think very little of our own constant sinning against God, we forget that our offences are, as the Psalmist says, more in number than the hairs of our head. If we are ready to forgive repeated injuries, we provide for ourselves the best ground for hoping for the pardon of our own relapses into sin.

The Book of Common Prayer speaks plainly and forcefully on this subject. In one of the General Rubrics (page 85) the parish priest is directed to remonstrate "with those betwixt whom he perceiveth malice and hatred to reign; not suffering them to be partakers of the Lord's Table, until he know them to be reconciled." Similar teaching is given in the second Exhortation (page 87):

And if ye shall perceive your offences to be such as are not only against God, but also against your neighbours; then ye shall reconcile yourselves unto them; being ready to make restitution and satisfaction, according to the uttermost of your powers, for all injuries and wrongs done by you to any other; and being likewise ready to forgive others

[37]

who have offended you, as ye would have forgiveness of your offences at God's hand: for otherwise the receiving of the Holy Communion doth nothing else but increase your condemnation.

It is a pity that this Exhortation is not required to be read in Church much more often, for it voices a necessary warning. It is by no means an uncommon thing for Church members, sometimes even for Church workers, to kneel side by side to receive the Blessed Sacrament when they have quarrelled violently, and are not on speaking terms. Fellow-communicants to be at enmity? It is unthinkable! Members of the same Body, disciples of the same Master, inheritors of the same Kingdom, stones of the same building, redeemed by the same Agony, regenerated by the same water, incorporated in the same Church, fed with the same holy Food—what excuse can they possibly have for remaining estranged from one another? "I don't feel as if I could forgive him," perhaps you say. "He treated me so badly, and said such bitter things and acted so unkindly; I don't want to have anything more to do with Him." He was a very bad fellow, no doubt; but then, *so are you*. Badly as he has behaved to you, you have behaved far worse to your Lord. After such forgiveness as you have received, you will indeed be a wicked servant if you withhold forgiveness from your brother. Remember your own illimitable failures—your constant relapses into sin, your ingratitude, your swiftness to judge others harshly; and forgive as you hope to be forgiven.

5

Tittle-Tattle

UNKIND gossip is one of the commonest sins of religious people, and one which we are, as a rule, very ready to condone both in ourselves and others, unless, of couse, we happen to be the victims of it. Many Christians who are otherwise good and kind-hearted constantly indulge in it, their consciences never condemn them for it, they never confess it, they make no effort to resist the temptations to it. Even when they discover that their tittle-tattle has caused great pain and distress, it is difficult to make them realize their responsibility for the mischief they have caused. They will tell you that "it was all a misunderstanding," that "they meant no harm," that it was the fault of somebody else who repeated or exaggerated what they said, and they will feel perfectly satisfied with such excuses.

The Greek from which the word "devil" is derived means literally traducer or slanderer. When we consider the immense amount of misery spiteful gossip has produced, the misunderstanding and strife that have resulted from it, the reputations it has ruined, the friendships it has wrecked, the congregations it has rent asunder, surely we must admit that it is diabolical, and that St. James is guilty of no exaggeration when he says of the evil-speaking tongue that it "is set on fire of hell."

Holy Scripture contains many denunciations of this sin. Thus, the Psalmist says of his calumniators: "Adders' poison is under their lips." In the Book of Proverbs we read: "Where no wood is, there the fire goeth out: so where there is no tale-bearer the strife ceaseth." And, again, "The words of a tale-bearer are as wounds." St. Paul in his First Epistle to Timothy speaks of idle women "wandering about from house to house; and not only idle, but tattlers also, and busybodies, speaking things which they ought not." It seems evident that St. James had had a very similar experience, judging from the stern language about evil-speaking contained in his Epistle, especially in the third chapter from which I have already quoted. He tells us that the reckless tongue is untameable, that "it is an unruly evil full of deadly poison," and that the Christian who fails to control his tongue is reduced to moral chaos. He has made himself the channel of hellish influences so that he cannot hope to offer to God worship which is acceptable: "If any man among you seem to be religious, and bridleth not his tongue but deceiveth his own heart, this man's religion is vain." And, on the other hand, "If any man offend not in word, the same is a perfect man, and able also to bridle the whole body."

St. Peter tells us that "charity shall cover a multitude of sins," by which he means, of course, not that it atones for our own sins, but that it makes us blind to our neighbor's faults. Using the word "cover" in an entirely different sense, we may say that tittle-tattle covers a multitude of sins, meaning thereby that it includes a whole catalogue of most unsavoury offenses.

The first of these offenses is calumny. Calumny is injuring our neighbor by making false charges against him, and it contains in itself two separate sins: it is at once a theft and a lie. The calumniator robs his neighbor of his most precious possession, his good name, and he does it by falsehood. On calumny that is *malicious* and *deliberate,* the *intentional* blackening of our neighbor's character by falsehood, I need not dwell; those who read this book are not at all likely to be guilty of it. Religious people who sin in this way generally do so through carelessness: they criticize other people and speak evil of them without taking the trouble to find out whether what they say is true, and without caring about the harm that may result. If we say something that injures another person's reputation, and it turns out afterwards, as it often does, to be quite untrue, we have been guilty of the sin of calumny and have incurred a solemn responsibility before God, whether we spoke deliberately or carelessly; of course the sin is greater if the falsehood was intentional. It is no excuse to say that we never meant to do harm, or that we supposed that what was said was true, or that we only repeated what was common gossip. *We are responsible for our words,* and for the unjust injury they have inflicted.

We may note here that to repeat lies about other people is almost as bad as to invent them. Indeed, many calumnies are made worse by the way they are exaggerated in the process of being handed on. There is always a temptation to improve on tittle-tattle, to add a few details which *might* be true, and so to touch up the story and make it more pointed and telling. Even if this is not so, and we pass on the calumny exactly as we have heard it without any embellishment (a very difficult thing to do, by the way) we give it additional authority, and share in the responsibility for it.

Another sin included in tittle-tattle is detraction. Detraction is closely allied to calumny, and differs from it only in that it does not include the sin of falsehood. It means saying injurious things about others when they are true and we have no sufficient reason for speaking. There is an old saying: "The greater the truth, the greater the libel." The reason for this is clear as soon as we begin to think about it. A man is likely to suffer much less harm from a false accusation than from one which is true or partly true, for in the former case it is far easier for him to defend himself. If, therefore, we injure another by speaking ill of him, it is no excuse to say that we were only speaking the truth. We must not give currency to true tales which are to the disadvantage of others unless we have very strong grounds for doing so. We are not bound to be silent about matters of public concern, or about circumstances where it is necessary that the truth should be known for our own protection or for the sake of others. But we must not speak about the secret failings or the misfortunes of others, even when we know that what we say is true, except in the comparatively few cases when less harm will be caused by speech than by silence.

A third ingredient in unkind gossip is censoriousness. The kindliest judgment, the greatest forbearance and restraint ought to be found amongst Christians, yet often the exact opposite is the case. It is not uncommon to find religious people who always depreciate everyone they speak about. They seem to have an incurable habit of saying something unfavorable or slighting about anyone on whom the conversation happens to turn. A critical spirit is a very poor argument for the Christian religion. "I do not call that by the name of religion," says Robert Louis Stevenson, "which fills a man with bile." The man in the street is of much the same mind with him. "Charity," St. Paul tells us, "suffereth long and is kind." It "thinketh no evil, rejoiceth not in iniquity but rejoiceth in the truth. Beareth all things, believeth all things, hopeth all things, endureth all things." If we are trying to be Christlike we shall put the best construction on the words and actions of others, and look at them in the most favorable light, remembering our own faults and failings, and forbearing to judge lest we should be judged in our turn.

Judge not; the workings of his brain
And of his heart thou canst not see.
What looks, to thy dim eyes, a stain,
In God's pure light may only be
A scar brought from some well-won field,
Where thou wouldst only faint and yield.

Tittle-tattle gives the mischief-maker his greatest opportunity. We are told in Holy Scripture that the sow-
ing of discord among brethren is one of the seven
things which the Lord hateth. Gossip would do comparatively little harm if it were not for the mischief-
makers who take a delight in going from one person
to another and repeating all the disagreeable things that
have been said. Such people generally pride themselves
on their candor. They tell you "for your own good" and
"because they think you ought to know what is being
said," and under the appearance of frank and open
friendliness they hide their pleasure in giving pain.
Thus what would have mattered little, if there had
been no "candid friend" to report it, becomes a fruitful
cause of misunderstanding and estrangement. "The
tongue of a busybody," says Bishop Hall, "is like the
tails of Samson's foxes; it carries firebrands, and is
enough to set the whole field of the world in a flame."
Most of the quarrels between friends are caused by mis-
chief-makers. Words spoken carelessly and in haste,
interpreted in a far worse sense than that in which they
were meant, separated from the context which would
have deprived them of their sting, exaggerated, and

told with an air of sympathy to the last person who should have heard them—how often such words have estranged hearts that loved each other well, and have been followed by life-long enmity!

Let me end this chapter with three practical suggestions. First, never listen to tittle-tattle if you can avoid it. If you are deaf, the tale-bearer will soon be dumb. When King Arthur enrolled his knights of the Round Table, he made them take an oath, "To speak no slander, no, nor listen to it." Especially beware of listening to gossip when you are told that what is said to you is "in confidence." How can you possibly believe a story told you by a man who has the effrontery to ask you not to repeat to others what he does not mind repeating to you? If he is guilty of betraying a trust, he is just as likely to be guilty of saying what is not true.

Secondly, even when you cannot avoid listening to gossip, determine that you will never repeat it. *"Nulla vestigia retrorsum;"* *i.e.* "no footsteps returning." That is the best of mottoes with regard to tittle-tattle. If needs be that it must *come* to us, never let it *go* from us.

Lastly, and positively, let us make it an unfailing rule that unless we have something to say to their advantage, we will not speak about other people unnecessarily. Let us see to it that we create in our own households and among our acquaintances a spirit of intolerance for tittle-tattle and a moral judgment that shall regard it as a mean and wicked thing. For ourselves let us resolve that if we have not something kind and favorable to say about others, we will keep silence when they are discussed. Such a rule we shall find by no means easy to keep; but unless we are doing our best to keep it, we are not really walking in the footsteps of the Master, Who has told us that for every idle word that a man speaks, he shall give an account in the Day of Judgment, and Who bids us prove our love to Him by showing our love to one another.

6

Depression

SOME time ago I was visiting a young mother who had that rain-washed appearance which made it obvious she had just been indulging in a good cry. She seemed so gloomy and depressed that I was afraid some serious trouble had befallen her, and I asked her if she had had bad news. "No," she said, "nothing is really the matter. I just feel utterly fed-up."

Here is one of those phrases of the street which possess a verbal precision that is almost uncanny. It describes exactly the mental dyspepsia which sours everything and takes all the joy out of life. I expect that most of us know the mood only too well, when everybody seems to be in a conspiracy to annoy us, and without any definite or tangible reason our whole outlook is shadowed in gloom, and life simply doesn't seem worth living.

The mediaeval moralists had a name for this temper of mind which is equally subtle and forceful. They called it "accidie," and regarded it as one of the deadly sins. The preachers of the time had a good deal to say about it, and it is given a dreadful doom in Dante's *Inferno*. It was prevalent in monasteries, and Cassian, one of the founders of Western monasticism, wrote an elaborate treatise about it. He defines accidie as a disgust of soul or weariness of life.

When a monk is first attacked by it (says Cassian), he detests the place where he is, and loathes his cell. He becomes critical, and thinks that his brother monks are unspiritual and neglectful of their duties. He dwells much on the excellence of other and distant monasteries; and the more distant they are, the more excellent he thinks them. He pictures to himself the pleasant and profitable life there; whereas all that immediately surrounds him is harsh and distasteful.

In those days, as I have said, accidie was regarded as a grave sin, and it would be well if we so regarded it today, as a cowardly and faithless discontent which will disappear when the spirit within rises up and defies it.

Accidie is certainly one of the sins which is "admired of many" today. It is, indeed, the characteristic temper of our time, and I am persuaded that it lies at the root of most of the troubles from which mankind is suffering. The whole world is a depressed area, and it is a superficial mistake to suppose that the depression is merely or even mainly economic or political. Behind the international discord and other secular dislocations there is a psychological depression, a spiritual *malaise,* a wellnigh universal feeling of discontent and disillusionment which destroys confidence and paralyzes effort. As the tides of the two World Wars recede farther and farther into the distance, the more apparent becomes the spiritual desolation they have wrought; and among the debris they have left behind on the shores of civilization is nothing more pathetic than the wreckage of hope. Permeating our art and literature and popular thought is the prevalent sense of the essential meaningless and futility of life. Into whatever company we may go we are likely to find the apostles of despair; the men who count the clouds till they say there is no sunshine, who count the chances of further war till they say there is no hope of peace, who count the sicknesses of civilization till they say it has no health, who count the follies of statesmanship till they say it has no wisdom, who count the failures of religion till they say it has no success, who count the troubles of life till they say it is not worth living. Where, for example, could one find a more complete expression of accidie than in these words of an American novelist, the late Theodore Dreiser?

I find life to be not only a complete illusion or mirage which changes and so escapes or eludes one at every point, but the most amazing fanfare of purely temporary and always changing, and, in the main, clownish and ever ridiculous interests that it has ever been my lot to witness. . . . In short, I catch no meaning from all I have seen, and pass quite as I came, confused and dismayed.

The belief that existence, for all its effort, has no

ultimate meaning or purpose; that the world is hurrying forward to the dark; that the wheel is coming full circle, and that civilization is destined to collapse: the poisonous current of this conviction runs through much of our modern thinking, and is destroying the courage and morale of people everywhere.

It thus becomes our urgent and insistent duty to conquer depression in ourselves, and to cultivate hopefulness as an antidote to the fashionable pessimism of our time. For, be it remembered, hope like despair is infectious. If there is a general depression it is only because there are innumerable individual depressions; and if there is to be a general return to hopefulness it will only be when there are once again large numbers of hopeful people. Every Christian ought to be a center of hopefulness, infecting all who come in contact with him with new confidence and courage. Indeed, he must be so if he is to be a Christian in any real sense of the word; a despairing Christian is a contradiction in terms. Hope in its fullest sense, as a supernatural virtue entirely distinct from the merely natural hopefulness of a sanguine disposition or the false optimism which refuses to face unpleasant facts, is a product of the Christian religion. It is part of the view of life which was brought into the world as a new revelation by Jesus Christ. To the pagan, hope was nothing but an illusion, a desert mirage, valuable perhaps as a spur to action, but certain to disappoint in the long run. To the Christian it is an anchor of the soul, sure and steadfast, set in the solid and unshifting ground of divine revelation.

Consider the example of our Lord. If anyone ever had cause to be depressed and disillusioned it was surely He. He was filled with the passion to love and serve mankind, yet he was despised and rejected of men. From the hour of His baptism, athwart His whole ministry, there lay the shadow of the Cross. Yet hope was the star which went before Him, gleaming most brightly when the night was darkest. "For the joy that was set before Him He endured the Cross, despising the shame."

As with the Saviour, so in their measure with His saints. They triumphed not only through faith, but through hope—a faith directed to the future, a faith that as Easter Day followed Good Friday so good must always in the long run triumph over evil. They were troubled on every side yet not distressed, perplexed but not in despair, persecuted but not forsaken, cast down but not destroyed.

Count me o'er earth's chosen heroes—they were souls
    who stood alone.
While the men they agonized for, hurled the contumelious
    stone;
Stood serene, and down the future saw the golden beam
    incline
To the side of perfect justice, mastered by their
    faith divine,
By one man's plain truth to manhood, and to God's
    supreme design.

[51]

My purpose in writing this book is positive and constructive. I have not only set myself to the task of describing the sins to which we religious folk are specially prone, and of pointing out their dangers—all that is comparatively easy; but I have also to suggest the ways in which they can be overcome—and that is very much more difficult. It is particularly difficult with regard to depression, because it is so vague and indefinite a thing. If it were some positive difficulty, we could face up to it and grapple with it. As a rule, like the woman whose case I described at the beginning of this chapter, we would be hard put to it to say why we get so depressed; and it is precisely this vagueness that makes depression so difficult to deal with. I do not profess to be able to prescribe an infallible specific which will meet the needs of every case and every temperament; but at least I can suggest some long-established and well-tried remedies which will be of real help to us in our hours of discouragement, and, if employed regularly, will usually effect a cure.

First, we must take care of our health. Our bodies and minds and souls are not separate and detached. We live a complete rounded life in which one part of our complex nature profoundly influences another, and a low-toned condition of mental and spiritual life may be, and often is, due to a low-toned condition of physical life. I have pointed out already that depression is a kind of mental indigestion; certainly it is very often the result of physical indigestion. We feel "fed-up" because quite literally we are fed-up, and a dose of medicine or regular exercise may work an entire revolution in our spiritual outlook. I have heard a story of a penitent who once came to a wise old priest in a state of great wretchedness and despondency. "Oh! father," he said, "do you know of any cure for a trouble like mine?" "A cold bath taken regularly every morning!" was the unexpected reply.

Secondly, we must realize that depression is a sin. We are much too apt to make excuses for it, to put the blame on ill-health, or temperament, or trouble of one kind or another, and to treat it as something which is quite outside the normal control of the will. It is true, as we have just seen, that for all of us at times "the corruptible body presseth down the soul"; and into most lives there come sooner or later troubles and difficulties that sorely tax the faith and endurance of the bravest. But though they tax us, they need not and ought not to overcome us. We may have a constitutional tendency to depression, or there may be many circumstances tempting us to give way to it, but we can check and thwart it by self-mastery, just as we can give free course to it by weakness and self-indulgence. To say that we cannot get the better of our moods is to contradict universal and everyday experience, and to deny the power of grace to discipline and strengthen the will. When once we have lost faith in our capacity to be and to do what God means us, and Christ gives us strength, to be and to do, we are done for—spiritually.

Thirdly, we must avoid talking about depressing things. The science of psychology has taught us a great deal about autosuggestion, the process whereby, through means of our conscious mind, an idea is implanted in the unconscious mind and left to develop there. It seems to be generally agreed that the spoken word is a powerful factor in autosuggestion, and that our mental outlook is influenced profoundly, though unconsciously, by the things we talk about. A good many people seem to take a ghoulish delight in talking about misfortune; illnesses, accidents, bereavements, troubles of one kind and another form their conversational stock-in-trade. Let us remember that such talk has its powerful mental reactions both on ourselves and on others. When you are depressed try not to talk about your despondency, and avoid expressing your mood outwardly. It is related of Ian Maclaren that, like many people of Celtic strain, he was subject to curious fits of depression and gloom which did not seem in any way to be connected either with his circumstances or with his bodily health. "But," says his biographer, "he never inflicted his melancholy moods on his family. He was only very quiet and absorbed, and kept more closely to his study. In a day or two he would emerge again, like a man coming out into the sunshine."

Fourthly, we must fight against self-absorption. In the last analysis, all the causes of depression may be reduced to one, egotism. We get low-spirited because we think too much about ourselves, our health, our spiritual state, our circumstances, our troubles. If, when depressed, we project our thoughts away from ourselves and try to sympathize with and help someone who is in real distress, we shall find that the hole out of which we pull our neighbor will be the grave in which we bury our own gloom. This was Keble's cure for melancholy. "When you feel yourself overpowered," he said, "the best way is to go out and do something kind to someone or other." This remedy has been expressed in memorable words which may be commended as a daily motto to all who suffer from low spirit: "Look up, not down; look forward, not back; look out, not in; and lend a hand."

Fifthly, let us cultivate a spirit of thankfulness. I shall have more to say about this in a later chapter, but here let me only remark that there is a credit as well as a debit side to life's balance-sheet, and that we are exceptional people indeed if our blessings do not far outnumber our discouragements:

> There are nettles everywhere,
> But tall green grasses are more common still,
> The blue of heaven is larger than the cloud.

The thankful remembrance of God's mercies to us will shame our faithlessness, and encourage us to trust that the dark hour through which we are passing is not the twilight after the sunset, but the twilight before the dawn.

Finally, let us remember the blessed power that

comes through prayer. Nothing so quickens the spirit of prayer as the feeling of discouragement. Nothing can compare with prayer as a cure for low spirits, for prayer links us to Him Who has said: "Come unto Me all ye that are weary and heavy laden, and I will refresh you," and in Whose bright lexicon of duty there is no such word as "fail."

At a meeting of the British Medical Association years ago, Dr. Hyslop, the superintendent of the famous Bethlehem Hospital for Mental Diseases, said a striking thing in this connection:

As one whose whole life has been concerned with the sufferings of the mind, I give it as my experience that of all the hygienic measures to counteract disturbed sleep, depressed spirits, and all the miserable results of a mind diseased, I would undoubtedly give the first place to prayer. Let there be a habit of nightly communion with God, not as a mere mendicant or repeater of the words of others, but as an individual who submerges his personality in the greater whole, and such a habit will do more to clean the mind and strengthen the soul than any other therapeutic agent known to me.

Words from such a source, spoken on such an occasion, come to us with an authority all their own. Prayer is an inexpensive medicine, and for that reason it is often despised; but it is not an easy medicine to take— it requires a strong faith and a disciplined will. Yet, when so taken, it never fails. No troubles, even the very greatest, can crush or dispirit us, if only we seek our strength from God in the sure confidence that underneath us are His everlasting arms, and that He will guide and guard us through all the trials and difficulties of our earthly journey, "till the daybreak, and the shadows flee away."

> Many a foe is a friend in disguise,
> Many a trouble a blessing most true,
> Helping the heart to be happy and wise
> With love ever precious, and joys ever new.

7

Anxiety

G. K. CHESTERTON once remarked in a fine phrase that whereas it was commonly supposed that Christianity had been tried and found wanting, the real truth was that it had been found difficult and had not been tried. That aphorism is capable of many applications, but it finds its most obvious illustration in our common failure to *apply* our religion to the problems of our daily living. Few of us, if any, live up to the full measure of our faith; and most of us tend to think of Christianity too exclusively as a system of worship and doctrine, and too little as a life. It is easy to come to Church, and join in worship, but it is difficult to live like a Christian; and most of us must needs confess how often and how completely our religion seems to break down in the very places and at the very times when it ought to prove our staff and our stay.

A familiar instance of this tendency to keep faith and conduct, profession and practice, in separate compartments, is to be found in the fact that so few of us suc-ceed in ridding ourselves of the company of "the old hag Care." Here, if anywhere, ought to be the most marked difference between the Christian and the non-Christian. Into every life come many things calculated to cause anxiety and distraction of mind: great sorrows, perplexities as to duty, disappointments and losses, annoyances and hindrances, countless petty cares and frets. All of these tend to disturb the peace of mind and soul, and we cannot escape them. Yet there is no precept urged more often or more forcefully by our Lord and His apostles than that we should never worry, never let care oppress us. We are to live not with distraction, but with peace unbroken even in the midst of the most trying experiences.

Anxiety has been called the "misery-habit." Just as ill-temper is a perversion of the instinctive emotion of anger, so anxiety is a perversion of the instinctive emotion of fear. Fear has played an important part in the evolutionary process, and it seems to constitute the whole of forethought in most animals; for ourselves who are fortunate enough to live under the protection of ordered government there is as a rule no need for the exercise of this instinct in its original strength. Our surplus capacity for it can be either sublimated or perverted: sublimated, it becomes prudence or forethought, the taking of necessary precautions against trouble or danger; perverted, it becomes anxiety or fearthought, the morbid anticipation of impending disaster. The difference between the two is easy enough to recognize.

Forethought leads to efficiency; fearthought to ineffi-
ciency. A chemist, for instance, may have a sublimated
fear of poisoning someone by a mistake in dispensing,
this leads him to be careful in mixing drugs; but he
may develop a perverted fear that he is sure sooner or
later to poison someone, a fear which obsesses his mind
day and night, and renders him quite unfit to do his
work.

Most of us know (to our cost!) how easily anxiety
can become a habit, and how much time and energy we
waste in gloomy anticipations. We make the day miserable by forecasting misfortune to ourselves or to those
whom we love: the possible illness, the possible accident, the possible failure in an examination, the possible
loss of a job, the fire that may burn down the house,
the investment that may go wrong, the war that may
break out—the whole ghostly train of fateful shapes
which our anxiety conjures up to torment us and make
us wretched.

I write [says the author of an essay on this subject] for
those who fear forty, and grey hairs, and consumption, and
cancer, and death, and beyond all that, the chance of something after death.

Man [says another writer] is reared in fear; all his life
is passed in bondage to fear of disease and death, and thus
his whole mentality becomes cramped, limited, and depressed, and his body follows its shrunken pattern and
specification. . . . Think of the millions of sensitive and re-
sponsive souls among our ancestors who have been under
the domination of such a perpetual nightmare! Is it not

surprising that health exists at all? Nothing but the boundless divine love, exuberance and vitality, constantly poured in, even though unconsciously to us, could in some degree neutralize such an ocean of morbidity.

It will help us to realize how foolish and unprofitable a thing anxiety is, if we consider how often the event has failed to justify our apprehensions. It is a useful practice when we are worried to look back instead of forward and to remember the many occasions when our gloomy forebodings have proved to be hopelessly wide of the mark, when, to use the Psalmist's words, we have been "in great fear where no fear was." The trouble we anticipated with so much anxiety did not come, or came in such a form that we found ourselves well able to meet it. How foolish we were to worry ourselves into such a fever of apprehension about it! As the old proverb puts it:

> Some of your griefs you have cured,
> And the sharpest you still have survived:
> But what torments of pain you endured
> From evils that never arrived!

Add to this, that many of the things about which we worry most are not worth worrying about at all. It is strange but true that the trifling troubles of life are apt to fret us far more than the serious ones. During the First World War, *Punch* had a picture which depicted a soldier who had left his trench and was crouching on the open ground with the shells bursting all around him; the sergeant was calling to him to come back, and

he replied: "Not me. *There's a wasp in the trench!*"
How true that is in ordinary life!

> The heart which boldly faces death
> Upon the battlefield, and dares
> Cannon and bayonet, faints beneath
> The needle-point of frets and cares.
> The stoutest spirits they dismay,
> The tiny stings of every day.
>
> And even saints of holy fame
> Whose souls by faith have overcome,
> Who wore amid the cruel flame
> The molten crown of martyrdom;
> Bore not without complaint alway
> The petty pains of every day.
>
> Ah! more than martyr's aureole
> And more than hero's heart of fire,
> We need the humble strength of soul
> Which daily toils and ills require.
> Sweet Patience, help us if you may,
> To bear the frets of every day.

I do not mean that all our anxieties are about trivialties, or that all our troubles disappear when we approach them. Sometimes, indeed, our forebodings of evil are realized to the full, and sorrows come that exceed our worst anticipations; but even when that is so, no good purpose is served by worrying about them beforehand. Anxiety weakens us and robs us of courage so that we become unfit to meet the difficulty when it arises. What friction is to the working of a machine, worry is to the effectiveness of a human life: it impedes the free action of mind and soul, and weakens our powers of endurance and resistance. As Charles Kingsley well said: "Do today's duty, fight today's temptation, and do not weaken and distract yourself by looking forward to things which you cannot see, and could not understand if you saw them."

People who have a habit of worrying are apt to say that they cannot help it. Disturbing experiences come into their lives, and they find it impossible to shut them out. Such experiences come to all of us, but we need not admit them and surrender ourselves to their power. It was the saying of an old Puritan: "We cannot keep the birds from flying over our heads, but we can keep them from building nests in our hair." Similarly, in *Emma* Jane Austen makes Jane Fairfax say to her lover: "How you can bear such recollections is astonishing to me. They will obtrude, but how can you court them?"

There is such a thing as "courting" anxiety in reverie and imagination, and it is only then that it becomes a vital force. Tomorrow's trouble does not exist today unless our imagination brings it to premature birth. The temptation to anxiety is always with us; but temptation is not sin. It becomes sin only when we yield to its importunities, and admit it into our hearts.

What, then, is the cure for anxiety? St. Peter answers that question with his memorable words: "Casting all your care upon Him for He careth for you." Two kinds of care are here contrasted: God's care and ours; and there is all the difference in the world between them. God's care is Providence—His loving guardianship and guidance of our lives; our care is anxiety. The distinction is quite plain in the original Greek where two different words are used for "care" and "careth," and it is well brought out in the Revised Version which renders the text: "Casting all your anxiety upon Him because He careth for you."

"He careth for you"—that is the reason St. Peter gives us for casting our anxieties upon God. In so saying he is only repeating a truth which is central in the revelation of Jesus Christ. Moffatt translates "careth for you" by the phrase "His interest is in you." It might be rendered even more literally, "He has you in His heart." If we really believe that, we shall take our troubles to Him as naturally and trustfully as a child runs to his mother when he is afraid. This does not mean that we shall get rid of them altogether; it does not mean that the cares of my parish will be lifted from my shoulders, or that your particular burden, whatever it may be, will be at once removed; it does not mean that you will no longer be concerned about the future of your children (how could you cease to be so concerned, since you love them?). What it does mean is that God will share our burden with us. He will take both ourselves and our anxieties into His heart, and we shall be so lifted up and supported that we shall find our yoke easy and our burden light. We shall be able to say with the Psalmist:

"Why art thou so cast down, my soul; and why art thou so disquieted within me? Hope thou in God, for I shall yet praise Him which is the help of my countenance, and my God."

It is through prayer that we can cast our anxieties upon God, for prayer is the great conquering force against worry. Such prayer must be definite: we must bring the particular perplexity or apprehension and put it out of our hands into the hands of God, so that He may work it out for us. We must bring the matter to Him as we would take a broken watch to the watchmaker, and leave it to him to repair and readjust. Having taken it to God and put it into His hands, we are to leave it with Him. We are not to tell God about our worries, and then go on worrying as if we had never gone to Him at all, or as if He had refused to help us. That is not trust, but faithlessness. "Be anxious about nothing," says St. Paul, "but in everything by prayer and supplication let your requests be made known to God"; and then this result will follow: "the peace of God which passeth all understanding shall keep your hearts and minds through Christ Jesus." The word translated "keep" means "guard like a sentry." No doubt the idea was suggested to St. Paul by the Roman sentry who guarded him day and night, and from whom there was no escape. From that constant daily trial he learned to think of the unseen Guard Whose unsleeping vigil kept him from all anxiety and fear. That is the freedom from worry which he gained, and which we, too, may gain if we will pray as He did.

If we are thus to cast our care upon God, we must be willing to let other people cast their care upon us. "With what measure ye mete, it shall be measured to you again." (The anxious man is always the egotistical and self-absorbed man.) It is extraordinary how quickly we forget our own anxieties when we are trying to help other people. It shows that we were never meant to live self-centered lives. There are plenty of folk all around us who have very much better excuse for being anxious than we have. If we try to show practical sympathy to them we shall find that our own burden will be wonderfully lightened. To quote St. Paul again: "Bear ye one another's burdens, and so fulfil the law of Christ."

Last, but by no means least, if we are to cast our care upon God, we must be content to leave the future in His hands. We have to do that in any case, and therefore the wisest thing is to do it with good grace. In all probability the future will not be half so black as we paint it in our moments of depression; and if it is even blacker, it is in God's hands not in ours, and we shall not make it one whit better by worrying about it now. Our Lord constantly taught us to live a day at a time. "Be not anxious about tomorrow," He said, "let tomorrow be anxious about itself. Sufficient unto the day is the evil thereof." That is one of the great secrets of successful living. Many men are wearing themselves out before their time because they persist in living in tomorrow. "I learned, alas! when it was almost too late," says Mark Rutherford in his autobiography, "to live in each moment as it passed over my head, believing that the sun as it is now rising is as good as it ever will be." The only way really to live the Christian life is to live it a day at a time. In God's service we are only day-laborers. With tomorrow we have nothing to do. His command is: "Go work today," and his promise, "I will give you a penny a day." Each day brings its duties and its difficulties, but each day brings fresh supplies of grace to meet them.

> Build a little fence of trust
> Just around today,
> Fill the space with loving work,
> And therein stay.
>
> Look not through the sheltering bars
> Upon tomorrow;
> God will help thee bear what comes
> Of joy or sorrow.

We do not know the future; but we do know the God of the future, "Jesus Christ, the same yesterday, today and for ever." What He has been to us in the past, what He is in the present, that we may be sure He will be in the future. "His compassions fail not; they are new every morning."

8

Self-Satisfaction

NOTHING is more remarkable in our Lord's dealings with men than His gentleness and forbearance. He was always patient with people, even when they brought to Him what seem to us to be silly and unintelligent difficulties; He was always kindly and generous in His judgments; He was always tolerant of failure and imperfection; He was always ready to see latent possibilities of good where no one else did. His faith in the inherent goodness of human nature must have been sorely tried at times, but it never broke down. In Him Isaiah's prophecy found its fulfilment: "A bruised reed shall he not break, and the smoking flax shall he not quench."

There is a legend that one day when our Lord and His disciples were passing through a village they saw a dead dog lying by the roadside. The disciples turned their eyes away, saying, "Unclean, unclean!" But the Master bade them look and said, "There is beauty even here. See! Its teeth are as white as pearls."

Whether this story is historically true or not, I do not know; it is certainly true to the character of Christ as it is portrayed in the Gospel. He was always looking for the gold of life even when it lay trampled in the dust and mire; and because He was looking for it, He found it.

There is one exception to this which stands out in striking contrast to His habitual attitude: it is His treatment of the Pharisees. His language to them and about them is always marked by withering scorn and stern denunciation. He does not seem to see any good in them; He never speaks to them as if He expected them to respond to His call. To other sinners, even the most degraded, He never said a single word which would lead them to despise themselves, still less that would encourage others to despise them. But to the Pharisees he does. "Woe unto you, Scribes and Pharisees, hypocrites!" "Ye fools and blind, ye serpents, ye generation of vipers, how can ye escape the damnation of hell?" "Verily I say unto you, that the publicans and harlots go into the Kingdom of God before you." So, too, He says to His disciples: "Except your righteousness shall exceed the righteousness of the Scribes and Pharisees, ye shall in no case enter into the Kingdom of Heaven."

Such language, which, coming from His lips, sounds so strange and startling to us, must have sounded far more strange and startling to those who heard it. When we think about the Pharisees, we remember how Christ has shown them to us, and the picture of them which

He paints for us is so despicable that we are apt to imagine that even in those days the title "Pharisee" was a term of reproach. On the contrary, it was a highly respected and honored term.

The word "Pharisee" means separate, and the Pharisees were those who stood for complete separation from all intercourse with the pagan world. Their religious life was throughout a protest against a prevalent tendency to obliterate the lines which marked off the religion of Israel from the heathenism of Rome. This was the meaning of their peculiar dress with its tassels, its fringes, and its phylacteries. This was why they braved popular scorn by offering long prayers as they stood in the public streets and squares. This was the explanation of their long fasts and their constant washings; the fasts recalled events in Jewish history of which the heathen world knew nothing, the lustrations symbolized an ideal of moral purity which was completely alien to paganism. Thus it was that they "sat in Moses' seat," holding the chief post of honor in the religious life of the nation, were regarded as the great authorities on every question which concerned the worship of God, were universally respected and admired as the strength of their Church. None was more regular than they in attendance at public worship, none more scrupulous in obeying the letter of the law, none more exact in paying every tax for the expenses of temple worship and the support of the ministry. Their almsgiving was proverbial, their liberality unquestioned. The best seats at feasts and the greetings in the public thoroughfares were only a part of the homage which was paid by all to their high reputation and undoubted respectability. If we can imagine the startling effect which would be produced by an itinerant preacher addressing the House of Bishops, or a diocesan convention, or a general convention or a conference of clergy in language such as that which our Lord used in denouncing the Pharisees, we shall be able to form some idea of the amazement with which His words must have been received.

Why is it, we naturally ask, that Christ condemned the Pharisees in words of such utter reprobation? What was the fatal flaw in their character and in their religion which placed them in His judgment on a level lower than that of the publicans and harlots? It was the sin of self-satisfaction. It shows how different our moral judgments are from those of Christ, it shows that we do not commonly regard self-satisfaction as a serious failing; whereas to Him it seems to have been the most dangerous and almost hopeless state into which a man can fall. We have had occasion to notice in an earlier chapter that towards the sins we are most ready to condemn, sins of the flesh, sins of hot blood and passion, our Lord showed a peculiar tenderness. He never condoned sin in any form, but He was especially quick to accept the first signs of penitence from those who had offended against moral standards which are generally accepted. The sins against which He was most severe were the sins that are "admired of many," the cold inhuman respectable sins of the Pharisees, the hard, sour, religious complacency of men who trusted in themselves that they were righteous and despised others. "There is truth in the saying that the sin that in its malignancy slew the Lord of Life, was the sin of Churchgoers, of religious people, of the pillars of the Temple, who when Supreme Goodness stood before them, would not see it, would not allow themselves to see it, but in spite and hate and sheer intolerance struck it down and stamped on it."

Our Lord pictures for us the sin of self-satisfaction in the parable of the Pharisee and the Publican. In one of those vivid contrasts with which He loved to teach and which are so illuminating, He gives us a lightning character-sketch of two men who stood at the opposite poles of respectability. "Two men," He says, "went up to the Temple to pray." One was a publican. The publicans were the tax-collectors, and were regarded with peculiar detestation by the Jews. The Scribes held that it was not religiously lawful to pay any money to a pagan government, and thus the publicans who exacted the Roman tribute were, if they were Jews by birth, regarded not merely as oppressors of the people, but as apostates from the religion of Israel. In common talk they were classed with harlots and other notorious sinners, they were called "the wolves and bears of society"; and there was a well-known proverb that classed every tax-collector as a thief. We can understand, therefore, how it is that the publican, when he comes to the

Temple to say his prayers, does not dare to approach the Pharisee, but stands afar off. When he prays he has not a single word to say in his own favor, or a single excuse to offer. If he is not as other men are, it is only because he believes himself to be worse. According to the Authorized Version he says, "Lord, be merciful to me a sinner," but in the Revised Version the rendering is even more emphatic: "Lord, be merciful to me the sinner." The Pharisee was the saint of the age, but the publican standing afar off from the Holy Place, confesses himself to be *the* sinner. So little right does he feel to be there treading the sacred pavement that he dares not even raise his eyes to heaven.

How different is the attitude of the Pharisee! He stands in the attitude of prayer, he uses the form of prayer, but there is no prayer in anything that he says. In a vivid and startling phrase our Lord describes him as "praying with himself." His "prayer" is a soliloquy in which he congratulates himself on his good deeds, his fasting, his almsgiving, his freedom from gross sins, his superiority to other men, especially to his fellow-worshipper. Everything around him was meant to remind him that he was a sinner; before him as he stood praying was the priest offering sacrifice for the nation's transgressions, the altar of burnt-offering stood directly within his sight; look where he would, the whole Temple proclaimed itself a temple built for sinners. He could see all this and yet feel that it had no message for his own soul. He could see all this and ask neither for pardon, nor for mercy, nor for grace. He could see all this and in the unalloyed complacency of his own miserable self-satisfaction, thank God that he was not as other men!

Why is it that our Lord condemns self-satisfaction so mercilessly? He gives us the reason in the closing words of the parable: "Everyone that exalteth himself shall be abased; and he that humbleth himself shall be exalted." It is not that self-satisfaction is in itself a worse sin than dishonesty, or adultery, or extortion; its danger to the soul lies in the fact that it bars the way to repentance, which is the first step in spiritual progress. We read in St. John that when Jesus had healed a blind man, and declared that He was come into the world to give sight to those who were spiritually blind, some of the Pharisees who were standing by asked scornfully: "Are we blind also?" To which He answered solemnly: "If ye were blind, ye should have no sin; but now ye say, We see, therefore your sin remaineth." It is the same warning which is given in the Book of Revelation to the Church of Laodicea: "Thou sayest, I am rich and have need of nothing, and knowest not that thou art wretched, and miserable, and poor, and blind, and naked."

In every department of life the law holds good that self-satisfaction is the enemy of progress. In literature, in art, in music, in business, the man who is content with what he has done has shot his bolt; his day of good work is over. There is a story told of Thorwaldsen, the sculptor. A friend found him depressed, and asked the reason. He answered: "My genius is decaying. Here is my statue of Christ, the first of my works which has satisfied me. Up till now I have never come anywhere near the idea in my mind. I shall have no more great thoughts."

In the life of the soul this law holds even more strikingly, because here self-satisfaction is more absurd, more false and more dangerous than in secular affairs. It is a dangerous state to have no standard of progress; but it is far more dangerous to have a low standard, to be content with it, and to aim at nothing higher.

The Pharisees as a class have long since disappeared from the scene of history, but Pharisaism as a spirit survives, and the Pharisee still comes up to the temple to pray. He uses Christian language, he wears clothes of a Christian cut, he busies himself in Christian effort, he subscribes to Church funds, he abstains from meat on Friday, he fasts in Lent, he serves at the altar, he sings in the choir, he visits in the parish, he comes to confession and communion, he keeps the precepts of the Church; but everything he says, and everything he does, is rendered unacceptable to God because he is *satisfied with himself*. None of us may safely deem himself free from the pervading infection of the Pharisaical spirit. Its essence is not satisfaction in this or that particular feature of our religious state or practice, but in any part of it whatever.

What are the causes of self-satisfaction? How does it

come about that in spite of our Lord's stern warnings on the subject we can so tamper with conscience and extract its sting?

The first cause of self-satisfaction I have already mentioned. It is our common tendency to be content with a low standard. The Pharisee trusted in himself that he was righteous because he judged himself by the standard of his class, who imagined that goodness consisted in observing with scrupulous care the letter of the law. Similarly we are apt to judge ourselves, and to imagine that God will judge us, by the standard of public opinion. Here, for instance, is a man whose conscience is uneasy at times about the kind of talk that goes on in the factory or office where he works, or about certain sharp practices in his business that sail close to the wind, and who says to himself: "They all talk in this way," or "everybody does this sort of thing"—"I am no worse than anyone else!" He is drugging his conscience with the standard of his own making. Or here is a girl who is waking to the consciousness that her life is by no means what it ought to be, and who is beginning to be drawn towards better things. She finds herself quite popular among her friends. She is witty and clever and attractive, and says to herself: "I can't be so bad after all, when so many people like me." Her popularity makes her self-satisfied, and blinds her to the defects in her character. The chief danger to our souls is the sin that is "admired of many." What we have all to realize is that God will judge us not by the standard of public opinion, but by the standard of the Man Whom He has ordained, the Lord Jesus Christ. He is our standard, and there is no other standard for a Christian. When we look at our lives in the light of His teaching and His example no room is left in us for Pharisaical complacency. We must needs stand afar off with the publican, and echo his prayer: "Lord, be merciful to me, the sinner."

The second cause of self-satisfaction is formalism. Like the Pharisee we are too often content with cleansing the outside of the cup and of the platter, and of putting the emphasis on what we do rather than on what we are. It is commonly supposed that formalism is peculiarly the sin of Catholics (particularly Anglicans) because of the importance we attach to rules and forms and ceremonies. A man may be just as much a Pharisee in dwelling on the special spirituality of his worship in contrast with the care which others give to externals, as in dwelling on his care for reverence and order in contrast to the irreverence of others. Formalism may insinuate itself into a Quaker Meeting from which all forms are as far as possible excluded, as well as into a High Mass where worship is surrounded by the most ornate accessories of art and beauty. Its spirit consists of treating the outward observances of religion as an end and not as a means, and of self-satisfaction in fulfiling them instead of using them for growth in holiness. All such formalism is an abomination to the Lord; and no outward devotion or obedience to rule can ever compensate for unreality in worship, or evil that is tolerated in life.

The third cause of self-satisfaction is the neglect of self-examination. "Know thyself" is a precept of psychology no less than of religion, and it is particularly necessary for us Anglicans to lay it to heart, since sacramental confession is regarded as voluntary among us, and therefore there is no security except that of right principle for our practising self-examination. If we make a habit of examining our consciences regularly and honestly, it will be impossible for us to remain self-satisfied, for we shall come face to face with our hidden motives which are in general so much less respectable than our actions. Let me quote here some striking words which Dr. Hadfield writes in his book *Psychology and Morals*:

Our conduct is often determined by motives of which we are quite unaware. People who fondly imagine that they are actuated by nothing but a sense of duty are often surprised to discover that the real motive of their conduct is the gratification of some latent desire. The politician, of course, desires only to serve his country, the clergyman to preach the truth, the ascetic to practise self-denial, the doctor seeks only the health of his patients, the researcher the interests of science, the slum worker to uplift the masses, and the saint seeks holiness. These are the conscious motives. When analyzed, it may be found that the original motives which led them to these lines of action were—in the politician, self-importance; the clergyman, self-display; the ascetic, a shrinking from the responsibilities of life; the doctor, his reputation; the scientist, curiosity; the saint, self-righteousness; the slum worker, a social snobbishness, which urges him to seek the society of people amongst whom he will be "somebody." These are their *unconscious* motives, which originally determined their line of conduct.

Dr. Hadfield goes on to point out that these motives can be, and often are, sublimated by being directed to noble ends; but the fact remains that they are there, and just knowing that they are there is a certain cure for self-complacency.

St. Luke tells us that our Lord addressed the parable of the Pharisee and the Publican to "certain who trusted in themselves that they were righteous and despised others." Self-satisfaction always breeds intolerance. If we are sure that all is right with us, we are quick to belittle other people, to thank God that we are not as they are, to be intolerant of their opinions, impatient of their failings, and harsh in our judgments of them.

This is particularly true of religious converts. In their zeal for their new-found faith, they are often arrogant and contemptuous of those whom they regard as still walking in darkness. This, surely, is one of the ugliest forms that self-satisfaction can take. The claim to possess a monopoly of truth, always unintelligent, and ill-mannered, is particularly nauseating when it is made by those who have changed their religious allegiance. It is no sign that a man has come into a fuller light, if he disowns and dishonors the light through which he came to it. It is a poor testimony to his new-found faith, if he is contemptuous of his former beliefs, ungrateful for his former privileges, and scornful of the fellowship he has deserted. If a Protestant joins the Church, he does not do well to defame the mother who bore him. If you were a Protestant and are now a Catholic, the best proof you can give of your catholicity is by gratefully honoring the family in which you used to live, and through whose power you grew up and passed on into the larger knowledge in which you now find your joy.

I have read a story of a priest who went to a Christmas party given for children whose crutches, piled against the wall, told their own tale. When he left he saw a little girl outside who was crying bitterly. He asked her what was the matter, and she replied, "I can't get in because there's nothing the matter with me." To think that we have nothing the matter with us is the only door which bars the way to the feet of the Saviour. "If we say that we have no sin," said the disciple who leaned on the breast of Jesus, "we deceive ourselves, and the truth is not in us. If we confess our sins He is faithful and just to forgive us our sins, and to cleanse us from all unrighteousness."

Here, then, is a practical suggestion. When we find ourselves taking a Pharisaical pleasure in contemplating our virtue or our good works, let us recall that part in our past lives on which we cannot look back without disgust. We may turn it to good account if we summon it from oblivion to drive from the soul the hideous spectre of self-satisfaction. Of this let us be sure. Christ's condemnation of the Pharisee stands good for all time. He will not accept us if we come into His presence, trusting in our own strength, and satisfied with our own righteousness. It is for ever true, as Mary sings with us each night in her Magnificat, that "He hath put down the mighty from their seat, and hath exalted the humble and meek. He hath filled the hungry with good things; and the rich He hath sent empty away."

9

Neglect of Prayer

THERE is no greater argument in the world of our spiritual danger and unwillingness to religion, than the backwardness which most men have always, and all men have sometimes, to say their prayers—so weary of their length, so glad when they are done, so witty to excuse and frustrate an opportunity."

So wrote Jeremy Taylor in his *Holy Living* some three hundred years ago, and so most of us find to be true. Every priest knows how much easier it is to work than to pray, and his penitents are constantly telling him the same thing. "I find it so hard to pray." "My prayers are so feeble, so lacking in reality, so disturbed by wandering thoughts." "When I have been on my knees only a few minutes, it seems like an hour." Such confessions are often on the lips of even the most devoted and consistent Christians. How much more serious must they be, coming from those of us who are at best half-hearted in our spiritual service!

No doubt plenty of excuse can be found for a lack of

the spirit of prayer. In the hectic rush and strain of modern life, most of us have but little time (we think!) to spend in prayer with God. That, undoubtedly, is one reason for the neglect of prayer; but there is another, and a far more potent one, because we can always find time for the things we really want to do. A good many people, if they were to tell the truth, would say that they have given up trying to pray because they have been utterly disappointed with the results. There is the story of an old Nonconformist minister in a Yorkshire town, who was preaching one day with his utmost eloquence on the power of prayer: he suddenly stopped, passed his hand slowly over his head—a favorite gesture—and said in dazed tones: "I do not know, my friends, whether you ever tried praying; for my part, I gave it up long ago as a bad job." The poor old gentleman never preached again. They spoke of the strange seizure that had overtaken him in the pulpit, and kindly contributed to his retirement fund.

I knew him five and twenty years ago, [says the writer of the story] a gentle old man interested in botany, who talked of anything but spiritual experiences. I have often wondered with what sudden flash of insight he looked into his own soul that day, and saw himself bowing down silent before an empty shrine.

I do not believe that this experience is at all uncommon. It is in times of great trouble and difficulty that a man really sets himself to pray; and when his petition is not granted, or when he thinks it is not granted (for,

as we shall presently see, *No!* may be as true an answer
to a prayer as *Yes!*), his faith in the power of prayer re-
ceives a shock which shakes it to its foundations. Many
a mother gave up the habit of praying during our two
wars when the telegram came to tell her that the son
for whose safety she had prayed day and night had been
killed. Very likely you can remember some such experience in your own life. Perhaps it was when some one
dearer to you than life itself lay on the borderland of
death, when the doctors went out silently from the
hushed room, and you set yourself to pray as never
before. You did not say, "Thy will be done." You tried
to, but you could not. You prayed with all the passion
of a soul that shrank from the anguish of bereavement
that God would give you back, even for a little while,
the life that seemed to be slipping from your grasp. It
was useless. The soul you loved so much God called out
of this life, and your faith, which up to that moment
had been unshakable, crumbled into dust. At first you
were embittered and hostile, then you were indifferent.
It was a long time before you could pray at all; and
though you have since resumed the habit of prayer, it is
without the old confidence. Your unquestioning faith
in prayer has gone.

When we consider the problem presented by such an
experience, it is important to remind ourselves at the
outset that *petition is only a part of prayer*. Prayer in its
fullest sense is the breath of the spiritual life, the lifting
up of the heart and mind to God, the act and habit of

inhaling that divine atmosphere in which our spirits live and move and have their being. Besides petitions for our own needs and our intercession for others, prayer contains praise, thanksgiving, confession of our sins, and the consecration of ourselves to God. We misunderstand entirely the place and power of prayer if we imagine that it consists only in asking. What would we think of a child who never spoke to his father except when he wanted something? In the prayers of those who pray most and best, only a minor place is given to asking. The truest prayer expresses the fullness of the soul rather than its emptiness; it is the cup of blessing running over. A remarkable example of this is the *Confessions* of St. Augustine. From beginning to end the book is in the form of a prayer, yet it tells the author's history and declares his most important beliefs. Evidently St. Augustine had formed the habit of doing all his deepest thinking in the form of conversation with God.

Yet, remembering this, it remains true that petition is an important part of prayer, and that our Lord has given us definite and explicit promises that God will respond. "Ask, and it shall be given you," He says. And again, "Whatsoever ye shall ask in prayer, believing, ye shall receive." And, once more, "All things, whatsoever ye pray and ask for, believe that ye receive them, and ye shall have them." Our sense of bewilderment, when our requests are denied, is in proportion to the great expectations such words awaken.

Much of our disappointment with the results of prayer is due to what one of the most beautiful of our collects calls "the ignorance of our asking." We fail to realize that piety is no guarantee of wisdom, and that God knows so much better than we do what is good for us. We say, "Thy will be done" as if it were a nemesis that we must submit to as best we can. We are not unlike the woman on shipboard in a raging storm who, having asked one of the officers if there was any danger, and received the reply, "God's will be done," said: "Don't tell me things are as bad as that!" That great prophet Studdert Kennedy once said, speaking of his experiences as a war chaplain, that he was convinced that much of the prayerlessness among the soldiers was due to disappointment with the results of prayer which was not real prayer at all, but only a pseudo-sanctified selfishness. If we really believe that God loves us, and that His will concerning us is the will of a father for his child, we shall recognize, as I have already said, that *No!* is as real an answer as *Yes!* and often far more kind:

> So weak is man
> So ignorant and blind, that did not God
> Sometimes withhold in mercy what we ask,
> We should be ruined at our own request.

Would you grant your child's request for something you knew would be bad for him? Would a mother give her little child a red hot poker to play with if he asked for it? Our Lord's promises about prayer are clearly limited by the condition that our requests will be granted only in so far as they are good for us. To cite St. Augustine's *Confessions* again, he tells us how earnestly his mother, St. Monica, prayed that he might not go to Italy. She was afraid that away from her influence he would plunge even more deeply into licentious living. Yet it was in Italy that he met St. Ambrose and was persuaded by him to become a Christian. And so St. Augustine was able to say, "Thou in the depth of Thy counsels, hearing the main point of her desire, regarded not what she then asked, that Thou mightest make me what she ever desired."

Our Lord's own prayer in the Garden was unanswered in the sense that the Cup of Agony did not pass from Him; He had to drink it all. Yet in denying Him what He asked, the Father answered His prayer much more fully than if His definite request had been granted. The answer came in the power that enabled Him to endure the Cross and despise the shame, and so take away the sins of the world. In the very heart of pain He found both for Himself and for us all "the peace that passeth understanding." So it has been throughout the ages of Christian history. The martyrs who were burned, tortured, crucified, flung to lions, and visited with every imaginable form of pain, no doubt prayed as Christ did—that if it were God's will they might escape the suffering, the sorrow, the loneliness, the heartbreaking desolation of their impending doom. The answer came, not in their escape from agony and death, but in the power to face both with an unbroken spirit. Their perfect trust in God is an example to all mankind. "When we consider the partialness of our knowledge, the narrowness of our outlook, our little skill in tracing the far-off consequences of our desire, we see how often God must speak to us as Jesus spoke to the ambitious woman in the Gospel story—You know not what you ask." It would indeed be a sorry world for us all if our unwise petitions did not often have *No!* for an answer.

When we reflect on our neglect of prayer and our indifference to it, and the ignorance of our asking, we see the need to turn to our divine Master, as did the disciples, with the cry, "Lord, teach us to pray." He is not only the hearer of prayer, He is the teacher of prayer as well. He teaches us to pray not only by attaching His most precious promises to the prayer of faith, not only by giving us in the Lord's Prayer the model which all true prayer must follow, but also by the wonderful and inspiring example of His own life of prayer.

It may be wondered that our Lord should have prayed at all. If He is God, as we believe, how could God pray to God; or what was lacking in His nature that made prayer necessary?

A partial answer is to be found in the knowledge (as we have already noted) that petition is only one province of prayer, and by no means the most important. When we remember that prayer is nothing less than the whole spiritual action of the soul turned towards God as its true and adequate object, it is not difficult to understand why the Eternal Son should have prayed to the Eternal Father. In this sense the whole of the earthly life of Jesus must have been one unbroken prayer, but this does not altogether solve the mystery of our Lord's prayers, for many of them were undoubtedly petitions for help. "In the days of His flesh," says the author of the Epistle to the Hebrews, "He offered up prayers and supplications with strong crying and tears unto Him that was able to save Him from death, and was heard in that He feared." Such praying by the Son of God is to be explained by the completeness of His humanity. Though He was born not as other children are born of a father and a mother, but miraculously of a pure Virgin, He was truly human, living a human life, feeling human needs, suffering from human pains, working with human hands, assailed with human temptations. He prayed for strength, for comfort, for help, because He needed these things just as we do. If He needed to pray, being what He was, how much more do we need it, being what we are!

It is significant and instructive to notice how consistently the Gospels place our Lord's life against a background of prayer. For instance, clear indications are given that He never allowed anything to interfere with His morning and night prayers. We, on the other hand, find so many excuses for shortening ours or leaving them out altogether. We have to get up so early in the morning, or we are so tired at night. How was it with our Master? Here is what St. Mark tells us about His morning prayers: "And in the morning, rising up a great while before day, He went out and departed into a solitary place, and there prayed." It was a day, no doubt, when He knew that He would have to begin work early; and so He rose before His usual hour that He might have time to pray.

Then, as to night prayers, let me cite, as an example, the evening following that particular busy and trying day when He fed the five thousand in the wilderness. It had been a day of continuous and exhausting toil, after which, as we might well think, night prayers might have been excused or shortened, but our Lord went back to the mountain alone, and spent the greater part of the night in prayer. He sent His apostles on and they crossed the lake; but it was not until the fourth watch (*i.e.* between three and six o'clock in the morning) that He came to them, walking on the waves. Tired out as He must have been, He did not allow His weariness to interfere with His prayers.

We learn from the Gospels that Christ prayed in all the great crises of His life. It was so at His baptism: St. Luke tells us that it was as He was praying that the heavens were opened, and the Holy Ghost descended upon Him in the likeness of a dove. It was so when He selected His Twelve Apostles (an act on which the whole future of Christianity depended):

"It came to pass in those days that He went into a mountain to pray, and continued all night in prayer to God. And when it was day He called unto Him His disciples, and of them He chose twelve whom He also named apostles." So it was at the Transfiguration when He stood on the borderline between earth and heaven and had to make His choice between the path that led up to glory, and the path that led down to agony: "As He prayed, the fashion of His countenance was altered, and His raiment was white and glistering." So it was on the night of His betrayal when after His high-priestly prayer in the company of His disciples, He went out into the Garden to pray alone. So it was when He was being nailed to the Cross: "Then said Jesus, Father forgive them for they know not what they do." So it was in the moment of His death: "Father, into Thy hands I commend My spirit."

Our Lord gives us an example not only of when to pray, but of how to pray. The life of prayer is a secret life, and many of His habits must have lain beyond the observation even of His disciples: but on one occasion, in the Garden of Gethsemane, we are allowed to see Him in the act of praying. We can learn much by studying His method.

First, we are told that He left His disciples, and went farther into the garden into a quiet place by Himself. So we often read of Him in the Gospels. "He departed unto a solitary place, and there prayed." "He withdrew Himself into the wilderness and prayed." "He went up into a mountain to pray." Some people who have not a room to themselves make this an excuse for omitting their prayers, but our Lord sets them an example in seeking solitude to pray. Such solitude we may find in the House of God. Most churches are open now all day and every day, and we may find in them a retiring place, a sanctuary shut off from the thronging avenues of daily life, where we may be alone with God. On our way to work or our way home from work we can go for a few minutes into a church, and, kneeling in the presence of Jesus, with everything in our surroundings helping to dispose your mind to devotion, we can say our morning and evening prayers. It is much to be wished that our churches might be more used for this purpose than they are—used as refuges where we may find solitude for prayer, away from the manifold distractions of daily life. Like our divine Master on the mountain-top, in the wilderness, in Gethsemane, we may pass through the welcoming doors of the open church into a quiet place where the tumult of the world is hushed, and we may be alone with God.

Then we read that Christ kneeled down and prayed. "His *prie-dieu* was the gnarled roots of some olive tree in the garden." Thus He teaches us that if we would pray well we must beware of laziness in our bodily posture. Here, as in all else, the body had a great effect upon the soul. The attitude of kneeling, the clasped hands, the closed eyes, help us to avoid distractions and keep our minds fixed on God. It is hard to pray well, if at all, when we relax into the most comfortable attitude we can find or bury our heads in the bedclothes.

Again, our Lord is described as being in an "agony." It must have been exceedingly difficult for Him to pray without distraction with all the sin and sorrow of the world pressing upon His soul, with all the coming horrors of Calvary set before Him. He was in an agony, and He prayed "more earnestly"—more earnestly because it was more difficult. The Greek word translated "earnestly" means "intensely," and our Lord teaches us by precept as well as by example that intensity is the very essence of successful prayer. His parables of the Friend at Midnight and of the Unjust Judge, and His blessing on the Syro-Phoenician woman insist alike on the necessity of importunity in prayer; and importunity means not dreaminess, but sustained and continuous effort.

God, says an old writer, does not care for the arithmetic of our prayers, how many they are; nor for their geometry, how long they are; nor for their rhetoric, how eloquent they are; nor for their poetry, how beautiful they are. What He does care for is their importunity, how earnest they are. It was the saying of a wise and holy bishop that no man was likely to have much success at prayer who did not begin by looking at it in the light of a work to be prepared for and persevered in with all the earnestness which we bring to bear upon tasks which are, in our opinion, at once most interesting and most necessary.

Compare the blood-sweat of Gethsemane with our individual spasms of petition. When we consider how little time and effort we give to prayer, and with what carelessness and listlessness we say our prayers, can we wonder that prayer so often seems to us to be a disappointment? "Easiness of desire," to quote Jeremy Taylor again, "is a great enemy to the success of a good man's prayer. For consider what a huge indecency it is that a man should speak to God for a thing that he values not." Herein lies the necessity for fervent importunity in prayer—not that it is needed to persuade God, but that it is needed to express, and, by expressing, to deepen our eager desire for the good we seek.

As we study our Lord's example in prayer we are tempted to say: "Who is sufficient for these things? How can we hope to pray as the Incarnate Son of God prayed?" It is true, of course, that we can never pray as Jesus prayed, because we can never pray with a sinless heart, or enter into such perfect communion with the Father as was His. An ideal, though, is not the less valuable because in its completeness it is unattainable. An art student who copies patiently one of Raphael's Madonnas knows that his copy will never equal the original, but he knows also that he gains his skill by trying to imitate the well-nigh perfect work of a supreme artist. So with us: we cannot hope ever to pray as Christ prayed, but we shall certainly learn to pray far better that we pray now if we strive to follow the example of our Master.

Let us be sure of this: there is no art better worth the learning. A man of prayer, it has been said, is like a great mountain in the Alps. The storms gather around it, but they make no impression on its mighty base. Our eyes gaze up the mountain-side, but we cannot see its peak hidden far above among the clouds. So with the man of prayer: his feet stand steadfast on the earth, but his heart is hidden with Christ in God, far away above the puny storms of the world. The mountain is strong and immovable because it is rooted in the earth; the man of prayer is strong and immovable because he is rooted in heaven, because his soul is linked to the mighty heart of Him whose strength perfects our weakness.

I end this chapter with some moving and eloquent words of that great teacher and man of prayer, Canon Liddon:

A time will probably come to most of us, if it has not come to some already, when we shall wish that the hours at our command, during the short day of life, had not been disposed of as they have. After all, this world is a poor thing to live for, when the next is in view. Whatever be their claims, created beings have no business to be sitting on that highest throne within the soul that belongs to the Creator. Yet, for all that, too often do they sit there. And time is passing. Of that priceless gift of time, how much will one day be seen to have been lost; how ruinous shall we deem our investment of this our most precious stock! How many interests, occupations, engagements, friendships—I speak not of the avowed ways of "killing time" as it is termed with piteous accuracy—will be then regarded as so many precautions for building our house upon the sand; as only so many expedients for assuring our failure to encompass the true end of our existence! It may not now seem possible that we should ever think thus. Life is like the summer's day; and in the fine fresh morning we do not realize the noonday heat, and at noon we do not think of the shadows lengthening across the plain, and of the setting sun, and of the advancing night. Yet, to each and all, the sunset comes at last; and those who have made most of the day are not unlikely to reflect most bitterly how little they have made of it. Upon whatever else they may look back with thankfulness or with sorrow, it is certain they will regret no omissions of duty more keenly than neglect of prayer; they will prize no hours more highly than those which have been passed, whether in private or in public, before that Throne of Justice and of Grace upon which they hope to gaze throughout eternity.

10

Ingratitude

EVERY one who travels along the roads is familiar with the different traffic signs, warning of crossroads, hidden lanes, rail crossings, road repairs, sharp curves, narrow bridges, etc. They tell of possible dangers, and one is utterly foolish not to keep his eyes open to avoid risking his life. This chapter is intended as a warning notice against such a perilous place. It is not marked in any map or road-book, yet it is always near at hand. Our own front door sometimes opens on to it, and our own street often leads into it. It is called Forgetful Green, and John Bunyan tells us all about it in the second part of the *Pilgrim's Progress*. When Christiana with her children followed her husband along the road leading from the City of Destruction to the Celestial City, she came to the Valley of Humiliation where he had his terrible encounter with the fiend; and one of her boys, Samuel, asked Greatheart, their guide, where exactly the famous struggle took place.

"Your father," said Greatheart, "had that battle with Apollyon at a place yonder before us, in a narrow passage, just beyond Forgetful Green. And indeed that place is the most dangerous place in all these parts. For if at any time the pilgrims meet with any brunt, it is when they forget what favours they have received, and how unworthy they are of them."

It is instructive to look up the word "forget" in a concordance and to notice how many warnings the Bible contains against the dangers of Forgetful Green. "Beware lest thou forget all the way which the Lord God hath led thee" is the constantly recurring motif of the Book of Deuteronomy. In the Psalms the same warning is taken up and persistently repeated. Take, for instance, the opening words of Psalm ciii:

Praise the Lord, O my soul; and all that is within me, praise his holy Name. Praise the Lord, O my soul, and forget not all his benefits: who forgiveth all thy sin, and healeth all thine infirmities; who saveth thy life from destruction, and crowneth thee with mercy and loving-kindness; who satisfieth thy mouth with good things, making thee young and lusty as an eagle.

Or turn to Psalm cvi which is concerned almost entirely with the sin of forgetting God's mercies:

Our fathers regarded not thy wonders in Egypt, neither kept they thy great goodness in remembrance; but were disobedient at the sea, even at the Red Sea. . . . Then believed they his words, and sang praise unto him. But within a while they forgat his works, and would not abide his counsel.

So, too, with the prophets. Isaiah warns the people as they turn their faces once more from exile to Jerusalem, never to forget the great deliverance that God has wrought for them; and we find similar exhortations in the prophecies of Jeremiah, Ezekiel, and Hosea.

In the New Testament the spirit of thanksgiving is deepened and intensified. Our Lady's *Magnificat* is the greatest hymn of thanksgiving which we possess. St. Paul constantly reminds his readers of the great things God has done for them through Christ, and his own prayers are full of the spirit of thanksgiving. The author of the Second Epistle of St. Peter, in depicting the spiritual destitution of the man whose soul has become barren, withered, and blinded, concludes his description with the tragic climax, "He hath forgotten that he was purged from his old sins." When we turn from the disciples to their Master, we note how completely the spirit of thankfulness filled His life. "Father, I thank Thee," was the motto of Jesus. We remember, too, the poignant question He asked when the nine lepers He had healed strayed on to Forgetful Green, and only one, recognizing its dangers, turned back to give thanks to his Benefactor, "Were there not ten cleansed; but where are the nine?"

As with the Bible, so with the Church: it is constantly warning us of the perils of Forgetful Green. Our Calendar with its recurring cycle of fast and festival is a perpetual reminder of the great events in the life of Jesus. We gather together in the House of God on the first day of the week, not primarily to ask for fresh blessings from God, but first and foremost "to render thanks for the great benefits we have received at His hands." We set up the Cross in our sanctuaries and on our steeples, and sign ourselves with it, in order that we may never forget the great salvation our Saviour has won for us by His death. Above and beyond all else, the chief service of Christian worship is, as one of its titles (Eucharist) implies, a signpost to warn us away from Forgetful Green. "Do this," said Christ, "in remembrance of Me."

We should make much more than we do of the Harvest Thanksgiving services. It is true, of course, that in some places the "Harvest Festival," as it is called, appears to be the chief festival of the year, and the people who go to it ignore altogether Easter, the Ascension, Whitsunday and the other great feasts of the Calendar. This, of course, shows an entire lack of the sense of proportion. Man does not live by bread alone, and we owe God our humble and hearty thanks not only or chiefly for the fruits of the earth, but for all the blessings of this life, above all for His inestimable love in the redemption of the world by our Lord Jesus Christ, for the means of grace, and for the hope of glory. When all this is said, it remains true that the abuse of a good thing does not take away its proper use. Even natural religion suggests to us how right and necessary it is that we should bring our first-fruits to the Lord, and unite in praising Him Whose goodness covers the fields with grass for the cattle, and with herb for the use of man.

Americans have a great advantage in this matter through their "Thanksgiving Day" which is observed in remembrance of all God's mercies, spiritual as well as temporal. It arose in this way: When the New England Colonies were first planted, the settlers endured many privations and difficulties, and used constantly to lay their distresses before God in days of fasting and prayer. Continual meditation on such topics tended to make them gloomy and discontented, and disposed to return home. At last, when it was proposed to appoint still another day of penitence and humiliation, a common-sense old colonist said he thought they had brooded over their misfortunes quite long enough, and that it seemed high time that they should remember all God's mercies to them: their happy homes, the growing strength of their colony, the civil and religious liberty they enjoyed, above all the great salvation that Christ had won for them. He proposed, therefore, that instead of a fast, they should keep a feast of thanksgiving. His advice was taken, and from that day to this Thanksgiving Day has been an annual observance in America.

There is little doubt that a lack of the spirit of thanksgiving is a grave defect in the religious life of many of us. It is startling to reflect how wounded and aggrieved we are by ingratitude shown to us, and how few of us regard ingratitude as a sin. As with the ten lepers in the Gospel parable, so with the majority of

Christians: probably only one out of ten is grateful to God for His mercies in nature and in grace, and nine out of ten are more or less conspicuously wanting in anything that can properly be termed gratitude. Forgetful Green is a crowded place.

How does our forgetfulness of God's mercies display itself? One way, at least, is in the disproportion between petition and thanksgiving in our private prayers. (Our devotional books are in general lacking in this respect.) Some time ago, a correspondent wrote asking me if I could help her about thanksgiving. "Apart from the General Thanksgiving in the Prayer Book," she said, "I do not know of any thanksgiving prayers." I knew of only one book to recommend to her: *Sursum Corda,* an invaluable little book of prayers which contains thanksgivings for every day of the week; I reminded her, however, of the rich store of thanksgiving to be found in the Psalms and Canticles and in some of our hymns, notably in the more ancient ones. Our forefathers managed their prayer life much better. Here, for instance, is a beautiful thanksgiving from the *Preces Privatae* of Bishop Andrewes:

O God, for my existence, my life, my reason; for nurture, protection, guidance, education, civil rights, religion; for thy gifts to me of grace, nature, worldly good; for redemption, regeneration, instruction in the truth; for my call, recall, yea, many calls all through life; for thy forbearance, long suffering toward me, even until now; for all good things received, for all successes granted to me, for all good deeds I have been enabled to do; for my parents honest and good, for teachers kind, for benefactors never to be forgotten, for religious intimates so congenial and so helpful, for hearers thoughtful, friends true and sincere, servants faithful; for all who have helped me by their writings, sermons, conversations, prayers, examples, rebukes, and even injuries, for all these, and for all others which I know, and which I know not, open, hidden, remembered, forgotten: "What shall I render unto the Lord for all His benefits?"

The same thing is true about sermons. I have a large homiletic library, and have read more modern sermons than most people, but I could count on the fingers of one hand the ones that deal with the duty of thanksgiving. I have quoted a thanksgiving prayer of one bishop; let me add an extract from a thanksgiving sermon of another. It is Edward King, the saintly Bishop of Lincoln, who is speaking, and the rare teaching of this kind is my justification for the length of the quotation:

I will thank Him for the pleasures given me through my senses, for the glory of the thunder, for the mystery of music, the singing of birds and the laughter of children. I will thank Him for the pleasures of seeing, for the delights through color, for the awe of the sunset, the beauty of flowers, the smile of friendship, and the look of love; for the changing beauty of the clouds, for the wild roses in the hedges, for the leaves on the trees in spring and autumn, for the witness of the leafless trees through winter, teaching us that death is sleep and not destruction, for the sweetness of flowers and the scent of hay. Truly, O Lord, the earth is full of thy riches!

And yet how much more will I thank and praise God for the strength of my body enabling me to work, for the refreshment of sleep, for my daily bread, for the days of painless health, for the gift of my mind and the gift of my conscience, for His loving guidance of my mind since it first began to think, and of my heart ever since it first began to love. . . . I will praise Him for my family, my father and my mother, my brothers and my sisters, my home, for my husband, for my wife, for the kindness of servants, and the love of children.

These are but a few of the things we can call to mind instantly when we think attentively and reverently of our creation and preservation and the blessings of this life. But what shall we say when we think of our redemption and of the hope of life to come? . . . What can I say to all this but "Praise the Lord, O my soul, and forget not all His benefits: Who forgiveth all thy sin, and healeth all thine infirmities: Who saveth thy life from destruction; and crowneth thee with mercy and loving-kindness?"

Another proof of our ingratitude to God is afforded by the careless observance of Sunday which is so very common today—even among religious people. Many reasons are given for the neglect of Churchgoing: the general unsettlement of religious belief, the low standard of preaching, the rush and nerve strain of modern life, the plentifulness of automobiles, the call of the country to the jaded city worker, counter attractions like radio and television, above all perhaps the *malaise* and pessimism of our modern outlook, which despairing of everything else has come at last to despair of religion. These, however, are secondary and superficial reasons. Behind them all there lies the real reason: men and women are forgetting God. They feel no sense of obligation towards Him—they take each day's blessings as though they deserved them!

The word "Churchgoer" no longer means what it used to mean—a man who goes to Church regularly every Sunday; nowadays it too often means an occasional worshipper who allows any trivial excuse to keep him away. In this respect Romanists set us an example we should do well to imitate; they realize as too many others do not that Sunday worship is a religious obligation. We are apt to sneer at the Continental Sunday; my own experience when on holiday abroad has been that it is invariably observed much better than the English Sunday. In Italy, in France, in Portugal, in Belgium, in the Roman Catholic parts of Germany and Switzerland, I have always found the churches crowded at Sunday Mass. It is not by amusements but by neglect of public worship that Sunday is secularized. The real question about Sunday golf, or bridge, or other recreations, is not whether these things are wrong in themselves, but whether they take the place of the primary purpose of the Lord's Day, the public acknowledgment of His mercies. Has God any claim on our gratitude? If He has, how can we acknowledge that claim if we deliberately absent ourselves from the Christian Assembly and use, for more selfish pleasure, the day which He has especially asked us to observe for His remembrance and the recognition of His goodness? The real tragedy of our modern Sunday is not that it provides increasing opportunities for recreation, but that over it there lies, like a thick black cloud, the sin of a people forgetting their God, forgetting Him to Whom we owe everything, and on Whom alone their eternal life depends.

The meagreness of our offerings affords further evidence of the lack of the spirit of thanksgiving in our modern religious life. Christians in the Middle Ages had far less money than we have, yet they gave to God more royally and generously than we do. The Church of England, for example, lives largely on their benefactions, while we starve its missions, and are often forced to raise money for current Church expenses by rummage sales and bridge parties. In many of the new housing areas great populations are growing up with no House of God in which to worship and no priest to minister the sacraments; while in well-nigh every town and village in the country at least one spire rises heavenward as an enduring witness to the gratitude of our forefathers. As John Ruskin said in words which once read are not easily forgotten:

The cathedrals and the parish churches are the only witnesses perhaps that remain to us of the faith and fear of nations. All else for which the builders sacrificed has passed away—all their living interests and aims and achievements. We know not for what they labored, and we see no evidence of their reward. Victory, wealth, authority, happiness: all have departed, though bought by many a bitter struggle.

But of them and their life and their toil upon the earth, one reward, one evidence is left us in these grey heaps of deep-wrought stone. They have taken with them to the grave their powers, their honours, and their errors; but they have left us their adoration.

Gratitude, like mercy, is twice-blessed. It blesses him that gives as well as him that takes. In particular, as I have said in an earlier chapter, it is a sovereign cure for depression. The fog of gloom which seems so unaccountable, but which nevertheless is so real and so common, is speedily dispersed when we allow our hearts to bask in the sunshine of thanksgiving. It was a saying of an old divine that when he was beset by his despondencies he used to walk among his mercies. Just as intercession is the remedy for selfishness, so thanksgiving is the remedy for low spirits. I know of no better prayer in times of depression than the lines of George Herbert:

> Wherefore I cry, and cry again,
> And in no quiet canst thou be
> Till I a thankful heart obtain
>   Of Thee.
>
> Not thankful when it pleaseth me
> As if my blessings had spare days,
> But such a heart whose pulse shall be
>   Thy praise.

Of all the secrets that are worth knowing, none is more precious than the secret of the peace and joy of the soul. There is nothing that reveals to us more clearly whether that peace and joy are ours, than our ability to say with complete sincerity the words of the General Thanksgiving: "We bless Thee for our creation, preservation, and all the blessings of this life; but above all for thine inestimable love in the redemption of the world by our Lord Jesus Christ, for the means of grace, and for the hope of glory."

11

The Love of Money

"THE Church to teach and the Bible to prove" is a true and wise saying which finds an apt illustration in the fact that the Church numbers avarice among the seven deadly sins; for Holy Scripture speaks of this sin plainly, and gives many reminders of the evil and dangers it brings in its train. There is no doubt whatever about our Lord's mind on this matter. "Lay not up for yourselves treasures upon earth, where moth and rust doth corrupt, and where thieves break through and steal: but lay up for yourselves treasures in heaven, where neither moth nor rust doth corrupt, and where thieves do not break through nor steal. For where your treasure is there will your heart be also." "Take heed and beware of covetousness," He said on another occasion, "for a man's life consisteth not in the abundance of the things which he possesseth." And He went on to illustrate His words by telling the parable of the Rich Fool with its contrast between material prosperity and spiritual bankruptcy. Similarly, St. Paul wrote to St. Timothy: "The love of money is the root of all kinds of evil: which some reaching after have been led astray from the Faith, and have pierced themselves through with many sorrows." Moreover, the Bible warnings against avarice are given not by word only but also by many terrible examples. Achan, Balaam, Gehazi, Demas, above all Judas, the betrayer, who sold his Master for thirty pieces of silver: they are the leading figures in the long procession of money lovers who move through the pages of the Bible, selling their souls for worldly gain. The Bible proves what the Church teaches, that the love of money is a grievous sin, which, if persisted in, will finally kill the soul.

We are considering in this book the sins which religious people are most prone to commit. It is well therefore for us to remember that the love of money, which was the immediate cause of our Lord's betrayal, was the sin of a religious man. That Judas was religiously inclined is evident from the fact that Christ chose him to be one of the twelve apostles, and that he consented of his own free will to follow Him. Most of us were born of Christian parents, and were made members of the Church at our baptism without our own volition. It was not so with Judas. He answered our Lord's call, and chose for himself the life of discipleship at a time such a life offered no gain or credit, and when there was some risk of unpopularity and danger. This indicates that he had the capacity to admire goodness and the desire to associate with it, and that he was not lacking originally either in moral courage or in self-denial.

Moreover, Judas was religious in the sense that he associated with religious people, moved in religious surroundings, and shared in unique religious opportunities. He lived in the closest intimacy with Jesus. He heard the very words, he witnessed the very works which are recorded in the Gospels. He heard and witnessed many more which have not been so recorded. For three years he had constantly before him the example of that incomparable life which was then, and is for all time, the Light of the world.

Judas, then, was a religious man with great religious opportunities; yet he ruined his soul and betrayed his Master by indulging in the vice of avarice: the love of money eventually filled his thoughts and controlled his actions. It is important to notice that it was not the making of money, or the saving of money, or the possession of money, or the spending of money, which made Judas lose his soul: it was the love of money *indulged in* until it made him care for it more than he cared for conscience or for virtue or for friendship or for God. It is not money itself but the love of money which the Church and the Bible condemn so sternly. It is true that to our Lord wealth was an unimportant thing, the loss or gain of which could never be a matter of much consequence; it is also true that He even regarded the possession of great riches as a serious spiritual handicap, since it takes up time and attention which ought to be given to higher things, and thus places a man in peculiar danger of moral wreck; but Christ never said it was wrong to make money or to take pleasure in making it. Many of His parables, indeed, show how interested He was in the business life, and how much He admired the skill, the punctuality, and the risk displayed in it. He loved to see the servants of the absent master occupied at their business of turning two dollars into five, or five into ten. He loved the audacity of the merchant who, catching sight of the pearl of great price, dared to sell all that he had and make his venture. He loved even to note the shrewdness and enterprise of a bad man like the unjust steward, who measured the situation, and acted with swift judgment. Our Lord would certainly never have told such stories as these, if He had regarded money-making as intrinsically wrong.

Money has as much right to a place in human life as has any other gift of God, and the wise use of it can give great blessing and joy. In his *Window in Thrums,* Sir James Barrie told the story of "the son from Lunnon" who came home for his holiday. When tea was over Jamie took a piece of paper, crumpled it into a ball, and threw it into his mother's lap. It was a five pound note!

I do not know [wrote Barrie] the history of that five-pound note, but well aware I am that it grew slowly out of pence and silver, and that Jamie denied his passions many things for this hour. His sacrifices watered his young heart and kept it fresh and tender. Let us no longer cheat our consciences by talking of filthy lucre. Money may be always a beautiful thing. It is we who make it grimy.

It is true. Money may be the ugliest thing on God's earth, or it may shine like the gold in the streets of the New Jerusalem. It is the way we *think* about it and the way we *use* it, that make the difference. It is not money in itself, let me repeat, but the love of money which is the root of all evil. Avarice is a deadly sin for many reasons, and one of them is that it blinds a man to the true nature and meaning of life. It makes him think that his life consists in the abundance of his possessions. "What am I worth?" he says to himself, meaning thereby not, "Am I a worthy man? What is my life worth in terms of character? What is its worth to God and my neighbor?" Not that at all, but, "What is my bank balance? What am I worth in gilt-edged stock, and debentures, and rents?" That is exactly what was wrong with the Rich Fool in the parable. He thought he was worth what he had got, and that his soul could be made merry because he had plenty of money. If we imagine that our souls have the slightest interest in dividends, and savings, and profits, except to see that they are honestly earned and wisely spent, then our Lord says to us that we are fools.

Among the sins which the world counts respectable, the love of money is regarded as the most respectable of all. Indeed, according to worldly standards, it is not a vice at all; it is a virtue. If there be one distinguishing characteristic of our age it is this, that we attach an entirely exaggerated importance to wealth. We are apt to think that it is everything and can do anything, and that time not spent in acquiring it is wasted from the true business of living. The love of money is no new thing, but the absorption in it of about ninety per cent of human energy is a new and disturbing phenomenon. Take our modern life through and through and what unity can be found in its thought and average ideals except the desire for riches? Can we say that we religious people are in general more exempt from that desire than others? Is there the marked and obvious difference between Christians and non-Christians in this respect that there most certainly ought to be? On the contrary, is it not true, that we think it a right and proper thing to honor people for their wealth, and that we are almost surprised at any other standard?

Here, surely, we may find the crowning example of our deliberate acquiescence in the sin that is "admired of many." With most of us our religion hardly seems to touch our attitude to money at all. We yield to the passion of possession just as much as world people do. We, too, become its slaves; we let it rule and possess us. In our own lives it keeps us struggling and working from youth to old age, heaping up money, providing comforts, and gaining what we call security for ourselves. In the lives of those around us we yield to its demands and render our homage to the man who overpowers us with the bulky imposition of his wealth. Do I exaggerate when I say that the central ambition amongst us is not that we may be wise, and not that we may be good, and not even that we may be happy, but that we may be rich? Have we no secret feeling of envy for the man who could say within himself: "What shall I do, for I have nowhere to bestow my fruits? . . . Soul, thou hast much goods laid up for many years. Take thine ease, eat, drink, and be merry?"

The fatal result of making money the chief god of our lives is the starvation of our souls. The soul cannot feed on the things that money can buy. It turns away in disgust from the food we offer it. Like an underfed child it pines and dwindles, loses its vigor and vitality, and becomes an easy prey to every kind of disease. Starve your soul, and what have you left that is worth the having? What do you still possess, counted in the coinage of the only wealth that endures, the wealth of character? What will you possess when you stand at last, as stand we all must, in the fierce white light that beats upon the throne of God? Your car? You cannot drive it along that road. Your house and furniture and pictures and securities? You will have left them all behind you. Your body, on which you have spent so much money, which you have loved so well, and fed so daintily, and clothed so fashionably, and treated so indulgently? Can there be any more egregious folly than this: to concentrate on the accidentals of life and ignore the essentials; to labor only for the meat that perisheth, and to starve the soul that endures?

Once again, I turn to the *Pilgrim's Progress* for an illustration. Mr. Little Faith was violently assaulted and robbed in Deadman's Lane. When he recovered his senses and was able to investigate his loss, he found that his assailants had taken only his spending money. His jewels were untouched.

Our spending money will sooner or later be taken from us by "the old thief, Time," but he cannot rob us of our jewels, the treasure we lay up in heaven. In Florence, visitors are shown the doors which Michelangelo declared to be fit for the gates of Paradise. They are covered with noble imagery in bronze, and are still beautiful. Originally they were gilded, and Dante speaks of them as the Golden Gates. The centuries have eaten away the gilt, but the magnificent workmanship remains. Which things are a parable. We shall all lose our gold one day in Deadman's Lane; but the imperishable possession of Christian character will still be ours when the last of life's robbers has fled.

Do we love money? That is a question we ought to put to ourselves very strictly and searchingly in the examination of conscience, for avarice is a sin that is peculiarly skilful at disguising itself. St. Francis of Sales once said that though multitudes came to him and confessed all manner of sins, many of them of a grievous kind, he could not recollect ever hearing a penitent acknowledge the sin of avarice. The money-lover is always slow to realize his fault. It is disguised, and he does not recognize it. He calls it by pretty names: prudence, thrift, care for his family, and the like, and easily persuades himself that the world is right in regarding the love of money not as a sin but as a virtue.

Do we love money? How much do we think about it? That is a safe test as to whether we love it or not, for "where your treasure is, there will your heart be also." If our minds are constantly filled with the thought of it, if we lie awake at night haunted by the fear of losing it, if we are discontented with what we have of it, if we envy those who possess a great deal more of it, then we have good reason to fear that the love of money has a large place in our hearts, and we need to take to heart our Lord's warning: "Take heed, and beware of covetousness; for a man's life consisteth not in the abundance of the things which he possesseth."

Do we love money? How do we invest it? Do we feel any sense of personal responsibility for the manner in which our savings are employed, or do we care only about the safety or appreciation of our capital, and the amount of our dividends?

Most of us are not in a position to know much about the inner workings of finance, and impossibilities cannot be expected of us: but before taking shares in a company we ought at least to satisfy ourselves that the trade in which it is engaged is useful and not mischievous, and that its methods are honest and straight forward.

Do we love money? How do we use it? Do we remember that it is not ours to do with as we like, but that it has been entrusted to us by its real Owner Who will one day say to us: "Give an account of your stewardship. I put so much money in your charge; what have you done with it?" Do we use our money conscientiously, with the feeling that we are responsible to God for the way in which we employ it? A good many church people take tickets in the Irish Sweepstakes, and join in football pools. Apart altogether from the entirely different question as to whether betting is in itself morally justifiable, can a Christian defend in the sight of God his share in a vast organized effort to appeal to the cupidity of the public? Is that the kind of way in which he ought to regard his responsibility for the use of money? Again, how much of our money do we give to others? Is a fixed proportion of our earnings devoted to almsgiving, or is the whole of it squandered on self? Do we consecrate our use of money by love so that it becomes a means of doing good and a symbol of self-sacrifice? In short, do we realize that the one really important question about our money is not how much we have, or how much we hope to have, but what God will say to us when at last we have to give in our account of the way in which we have spent it? Will He say: "Well done: thou good and faithful servant. Thou hast been faithful in a few things; I will make thee ruler over many things"? Or will He say, "Thou fool"?

Do we love money? If we do, we ought to pray most earnestly for God's grace to enable us to overcome a sin which, however respectable it may be, is base and sordid, and utterly contrary to the mind of Christ. Avarice is a deadly poison, destructive of all virtue. It dries up the milk of human kindness and makes us hard, callous, indifferent towards the needs of our fellow-creatures, and it makes us miserable and discontented, too. The money-lover is never satisfied. He can never keep his thoughts fixed on what he has, but is always in another tense and mood, thinking of what he could, would, might, or should have. Let us not imitate the Rich Fool, but learn heavenly wisdom while we may. There are prizes on earth, there are treasures in heaven, more precious, more enduring, more worthy of pursuit by far, than the unsubstantial bubble of worldly prosperity, or the glittering phantoms of time. Yet "it is as the children of time that we are taking our measures for eternity. And, while time is short, eternity is long."

12

Namby-Pambyism

TO THE man in the street there is something weak and insipid about the Christian religion. If he is a psychologist he will very likely describe it as an escape mechanism, a means of seeking refuge from the hard realities of life. If he is a Marxist he will tell you that it is dope used by the "haves" for the purpose of keeping the "have-nots" docile and contented with their lot. If he is an intelligent pagan he will say that the type of life exhibited and demanded by Christ, so far from being worthy of admiration, is antagonistic to human progress. Some will say that it has no tonic power; that it is lacking in virility and strength; that its so-called virtues, meekness, humility, patience, long-suffering, are in reality vampire bats, draining from the veins of civilization the rich red life-blood of power. We have seen this view put into practice to our great sorrow in the rise of Nazism. Its prophet was Nietzsche, who wrote:

I impeach the greatest blasphemy in time—the religion

which has enchained and softened us. What have we to do with the herd morality which expresses itself in modern democracy? It is good for cows, women, and Englishmen. A new commandment give I unto you, my brethren, be hard. For the best things in life belong to us, the best food, the purest sky, the fairest women, the strongest thoughts. And if men do not give us these things, we take them.

In spite of our terrible experience of the application of this philosophy in our own time, many a man today, who would by no means agree with this wholesale condemnation of Christian moral values, is still nevertheless alienated from the Church because he thinks that the religion it preaches is weak, flaccid, and sentimental. Perhaps the virus of Nazism has found its way into our own blood stream. At any rate such a man feels that the tendency of Christianity is to make a man too much like a sheep. His idea of a clergyman, priest or protestant minister, is a "gentle" creature with hair parted down the middle, who always addresses people as "dearly beloved brethren," whose proper place is at a guild tea, and who (does not his cassock proclaim it?) is only half a man. Churchgoing, he thinks, is all very well for his children and for his wife after she has made the beds, tidied up the house, and generally attended to his domestic needs; but church is no place for a man.

The same note of impatience with a feeble and emasculated Christianity sounds in the passionate lines of a modern poet:

Jesus, Whose lot with us was cast,
Who saw it out from first to last,
Would I could win and keep and feel
That heart of love, that spirit of steel!
I would not to Thy bosom fly
To shirk off till the storms go by;
If You are like the man You were,
You'd turn in scorn from such a prayer.

Flog me and spur me, set me straight
At some vile job I fear and hate;
Some sickening round of long endeavor,
No light, no rest, no outlet ever;
All at a pace that must not slack
Though heart would burst and sinews crack;
Fog in one's eyes, the brain aswim,
A weight like lead in every limb,
And a raw pit that burns like hell
Where the light breath once rose and fell:
Do you but keep me, hope or none,
Cheery and staunch till all is done,
And, at the last gasp, quick to lend
One effort more to save a friend.

I am afraid there is only too much in our religion,
as it is still preached and practiced today, to give point
to the criticism that it is weak, wishy-washy, effeminate, namby-pamby, with no appeal to a strong, virile,
active man. Pleasant Sunday afternoons; sentimental
and subjective hymns of the "Art thou weary, art thou
languid?" variety; "goody-goody" sermons guaranteed
to offend nobody; modern religious art which under

the influence of Burne-Jones has substituted decorative effect for realism, and tends to represent Christ and His saints as weak anemic figures destitute of life and vigor; all this kind of thing has encouraged the notion that Christianity is not a religion for full-blooded people. It is true that there has been much improvement in recent years but the memory of earlier days linger, and we know that there is still too much of this debasement of the Faith.

I do not deny that these examples are superficial and that they represent a very one-sided view of the picture. I give them not only because they make us an easy target for the critics and the cynics, but because I believe they are symptomatic of the encroachment of an effeminate streak in our modern Christianity which imperils its native robustness and turns its blood to water. Can we possibly say that virility is a characteristic of our present-day religion, and that by the very vigor and impulse of our living we arrest the world in wonder? Consider, for instance, the feebleness of our moral witness. How nerveless, indecisive, and importunate it often is! We seem to be afraid nowadays of calling sins by their proper names. Lest we should give offence to anyone and be thought strait-laced and narrow-minded, we wrap them up in the silver foil of pretty phrases so that they look almost like virtues. To give but one example, take the question of marriage. No part of Christian witness could seem more vital to morality, more in line with the plain teaching of Christ than that which proclaims that Christian marriage is indissoluble. Our Lord does not mince His words on the matter: "They twain shall become one flesh; wherefore, whosoever putteth away his wife and taketh another committeth adultery, and whosoever marrieth her that is put away committeth adultery." Compare this with a resolution of the Lower House of the Convocation of York:

That this House, notwithstanding the existence of well-known New Testament texts which have been held to justify divorce for adultery, nevertheless believes that for a Christian man or woman to remarry during the lifetime of a former partner must involve always, in greater or less degree, a failure to bear the highest type of Christian witness to the permanence of marriage.

That resolution, with its hesitancies, and qualifications, and circumlocutions, and unwillingness to censure, except in the very mildest terms, Christians who have broken the solemn vows they made before the Altar of God, surely touches the highwater mark of namby-pambyism. Such a toning down of the ethics of the Gospel to make them acceptable to human selfishness and frailty, richly merits the derisive contempt of the world.

As with our moral witness so with our moral discipline. How vacillating it often is; how lacking in energy and resolution! Most of us have next to no conscience about our religious obligations either public or private. Sleepiness suffices to render our evening prayers very perfunctory indeed, even if it does not make us omit them altogether; and a shower of rain is sufficient excuse for neglecting the public worship of God. Think, too, of our modern observance of Lent. Is it an exaggeration to say that with the majority of us it is a complete travesty of what is meant by fasting? In primitive times the Lenten fast was observed with great strictness and rigor.

There are those [says St. Chrysostom] who rival one another in fasting, and show a marvellous emulation in it; some indeed who spend two whole days without food at a time; and others who reject from their tables not only the use of wine and oil, but of every dish except bread and water, and persevere in this practice during the whole of Lent.

We need not go back to ancient times or to another country to find an example of the proper observance of Lent. Here is a description by Robert Nelson, a prominent layman of the day, of the manner in which Lent was observed by religious people at the beginning of the eighteenth century, when spiritual privileges, such as we take for granted today, were unknown:

We cannot in these days endure the privations which the primitive Christians love to practice; yet everyone should spend some part of the time in fasting and abstinence, according to the circumstances of his health and outward condition in the world, and this with a design to deny and punish himself, and to express his humiliation before God for his past transgressions. The ornaments of attire may be laid aside as improper to express the sense of mourners;

and the frequency of paying and receiving visits may be interrupted as unseasonable when our minds are oppressed with sorrow. Public assemblies for pleasure and diversion should be avoided; we should be liberal in our alms, and very ready to employ ourselves in all opportunities of relieving either the temporal or spiritual wants of our neighbors. And we should frequently exercise ourselves in the meditation of divine subjects, the best means to make all discourses from the press and from the pulpit effectual to our salvation.

Do not those words form a striking and significant contrast to the Lent of the average Churchman of today? Even if we admit that the religious *regime* of our fathers is altogether too Spartan for our pleasure-loving age, ought we to be content to settle down into an easy-chair religion, in which self-denial, self-discipline, and asceticism are altogether at a discount? Surely it would help to put iron into our blood if we made the obligations of our religion more a matter of conscience, and an opportunity for the training of our over-pampered bodies. By the neglect of the severer side of Christian discipleship, we are in grave danger of losing its masculinity and of becoming soft, limpid, and namby-pamby. It has been found that a cause of softness in children's bones is the softness of water that lacks the harder elements, the lime that goes to the making of bone. In the Christian life, when the bones are too soft and gristly, or when the backbone is altogether wanting, the cause is often to be found in the ignoring of the harder and severer elements of Christian discipline.

It is not only in the feebleness of our moral witness and the slackness of our moral discipline that our namby-pambyism is apparent, it is to be seen also in the lack of decisive conviction that marks so much of our religious thinking. We seem to be approaching a time when the only people who will be entitled to be called broad-minded will be people who have no definite convictions at all. Needless to say, I am not pleading for intolerance. We who believe that Christianity is the noblest of all religions cannot serve it by striking a harsh and intolerant note. The more we believe in our own Catholic Faith, the less we can deny to other religions their measure of truth and beauty and power; but there is all the difference in the world between toleration, which springs from a real respect for the beliefs of others, and indecisiveness, which is unwilling to make any distinctive doctrinal stand. Christianity first came to the world, as its Master said it would come, like a sword. Its message was flung down in the face of the old religions as a provocative challenge. It utterly refused to accept a place for Christ in the Pantheon of the gods. It claimed that "there is none other name under heaven given among men whereby we must be saved, than the name of Jesus of Nazareth." Search the New Testament from end to end, and you will nowhere find a hint of compromise about the supremacy and uniqueness of Christ, and the necessity for seeking salvation through Him. That is the distinctive note both of our Lord's own witness, and of the preaching of His apostles.

It is the urgency of this conviction which we have lost and which we need so desperately to recover. We hear a good deal today about the recall of the nation to religion, and the part we ought to take in sounding it; but before we can give a message to others, we need to be sure about our own faith. Are we ourselves *convinced* that there is no other name whereby we must be saved than the name of Jesus? Or are we disposed to say, confronted as we are with other beliefs that are fast making a wilderness of civilization, that it does not much matter what a man believes? Talk to a Communist and you will soon find that there is nothing namby-pamby or indecisive about *his* mental attitude! His conviction prompts him to real effort and self-denial. Conviction has been the driving power behind all the great evangelistic movements of the Church during the centuries. *It is because we have lost it that we are being defeated all along the line today.*

A weak and flaccid piety is a caricature of the Gospel of Christ. Listen to St. Paul: "I therefore so run, not as uncertainly; so fight I, not as one that beateth the air; but I keep under my body and bring it into subjection." Listen to St. Peter: "Be sober, be vigilant; because your adversary the devil, as a roaring lion, walketh about, seeking whom he may devour: whom resist stedfast in the Faith." Listen to St. Jude: "Earnestly contend for the Faith once delivered to the saints." Listen to the

[128]

author of the Epistle to the Hebrews: "Ye have not yet resisteth unto blood, fighting against sin." Is this the language of sentimental weaklings, of kid-glove Christians? Does there not rather ring through it a passionate vehemence, a determined energy, an intense and concentrated resolution? Turn from the apostolic writers to the colossal Figure of their Master: Jesus Christ as the Gospels represent Him is no timid creature, sheepish and effeminate, with His hands clasped in pathetic and ineffectual appeal; He is an extraordinary Being with lips of thunder and acts of lurid decision, flinging down tables, casting out devils, spending long nights in lonely vigil upon the mountaintops, hurling denunciations in the teeth of the ruling classes, choosing the path of Calvary and going down it like a thunderbolt. His very diction is gigantesque, full of camels leaping through needles, and mountains hurled into the sea. His picture of the heavenly pilgrimage is not that of a gentle and languid saunter along a flower-strewn path of luxury; it is a passionate and exhausting march along a stiff and bloodstained track. "Strait is the gate," He said, "and narrow is the way that leadeth unto life; and few there be that find it." And, again, "the kingdom of heaven suffereth violence and the violent take it by force." As a landscape may be mirrored in a dewdrop, so here, in this arresting word of Christ, we see a vision of the Christian life as it really is: a task for strong men, an obstinate and venturesome siege, a storming of an almost impregnable stronghold.

As soon as a man really sets himself to follow Christ, he finds out that the Christian religion, so far from being namby-pamby, is a struggle, a conflict, a holy war, which calls forth all his powers of courage and fortitude and resolution. The Kingdom of heaven opposes him with a strange power of resistance. It does not stand with open gates to welcome him; on the contrary, it slams those gates in his face, bars, bolts and barricades them, and settles down to keep him at bay as long as possible. It will never yield up its treasures to the weak, the flabby, the irresolute. Its prizes are "to him that overcometh." To use Tennyson's expressive phrase: "It holds us off that it may draw us on."

I have quoted John Bunyan more than once in this book, but I cannot leave him out of this chapter, for more than any other book ever written, except the Bible, the *Pilgrim's Progress* is a sure prophylactic against religious namby-pambyism.

Then the Interpreter took Christian and led him up toward the door of the palace; and behold! at the door stood a great company of men as desirous to go in, but durst not. There also sat a man at a little distance from the door, at a tableside, with a book and his inkhorn before him, to take the name of him that should enter therein; he saw also that in the doorway stood many men in armour to keep it, being resolved to do to the men that would enter what hurt and mischief they could. At last, when every man started back for fear of the armed men, Christian saw a man of a very stout countenance come up to the man that sat there to write, saying: "Set down my name, sir." The which, when he had done, he saw the man draw his sword and put a helm upon his head, and rush toward the door upon the armed men, who laid upon him with deadly force. But the man, not at all discouraged, fell to cutting and hacking most fiercely. So that, after he had received and given many wounds to those that attempted to keep him out, he cut his way through them all, and pressed forward into the palace. At which there was a pleasant voice heard from those that were within, even of those that walked upon the top of the palace, saying:

> Come in! Come in!
> Eternal glory thou shalt win.

All who have *really* tried to follow Jesus Christ will recognize the truth of that description. At first it resisted and repelled us; perhaps it still resists and repels us. Gird up your strength, and fling yourself against the citadel anew! Say to Christ, as Jacob said of old time when he wrestled with the angel: "I will not let thee go unless thou bless me." If we will but do that, the result is sure. The gates will be flung open at our challenge, and we shall enter into possession of the unsearchable riches of Christ. There is no place in this holy warfare for the namby-pamby soldier. For "the kingdom of heaven suffereth violence, and the violent take it by force."

13

Moral Cowardice

MORAL cowardice is a symptom of the disease of namby-pambyism so prevalent and so destructive of spiritual vigor as to need a chapter to itself. Most of us regard cowardice as one of the most contemptible of vices and would indignantly resent its imputation. Nevertheless, it is so common as to be almost universal. We are not all physical cowards; on the contrary, physical courage is a fairly common virtue. War provides countless examples of it, every hospital ward gives evidence of it; we can hardly open a newspaper with its record of fire, wreck, and accident without finding proof that most men and women will face up to danger without quailing. But moral courage is a very different thing. To dare to do and say what we know we ought to do and say, in the face of a public opinion which condemns or ridicules us for doing and saying it, that is rare indeed. We may think we have moral courage until a test comes, and then we realize what a difficult virtue it is, and how sadly we lack it.

True, moral cowardice is not one of the sins that is "admired of many," but it is a sin that is practiced by most.

Just after He had forewarned His disciples of His approaching sufferings and death, our Lord told them of the judgment that awaited those of His followers who failed in moral courage: "Whosoever shall be ashamed of Me, and of My words, of him shall the Son of Man be ashamed when He shall come in His own glory, and in His Father's, and of the holy angels." We gather from the Gospels that these words came to the disciples as a complete surprise. They could not understand that the time would ever come when they would be tempted to be ashamed of Christ. They were proud of their association with Him. His cause had grown, multitudes followed Him, His fame was spread abroad everywhere, and the common people heard Him gladly. The Jews were looking for the coming of a deliverer who would free them from foreign domination and who would reign as a king in Jerusalem. The disciples had come to believe that our Lord was the expected king; and though He spoke one parable after another, and multiplied explanations and illustrations—all in order to teach them that His kingdom was a spiritual kingdom and not a mere realm of worldly power and dominion, to the last they continued to misunderstand Him. They looked forward with eager hope to the speedy establishment of His kingdom, and to their appointment to high positions within it.

It was not long before they learned how mistaken they had been, and how necessary was their Master's warning. It was not long before St. Peter had denied three times that he had ever known Christ, not long before all the apostles had forsaken Him and fled, not long before Christians were a persecuted minority who needed moral courage to enable them to be Christians at all. For the first three hundred years of its existence, the Church lived through an almost uninterrupted reign of terror. In ten great persecutions the whole force of the imperial government was engaged in a ruthless attempt to stamp out Christianity utterly. Throughout the greater part of that period when the authority of everything that has weight with men—rank, wealth, learning, and power—was stacked in opposition to the Faith, to be shamed because of Christ was to be like Him—despised and rejected of men and ready to suffer imprisonment or death for His sake. Wonderful it is how, in those first ages of the Church, men and women, boys and girls, in all conditions of life, joyfully accepted a painful death rather than be disloyal to their Lord and Saviour. As we study the ancient records we meet with the same story over and over again: "the popular suspicion of the 'crime' of Christianity; the denunciation; the arrest; the trial before the imperial officer; the refusal; the official expostulation; the second refusal; the threats, more and more terrifying, in order to break down what seemed an irrational obstinacy; the final triumph of conscience, which calmly and deliberately would accept the worst rather than be false to truth; and then the last dark scenes of agony until all had closed in death." When all the world was against the Gospel; when everyone took it for granted that Christianity was the most fantastic folly, and that those who believed in it were the most stupid and obstinate of bigots; when at every turn men were likely to be mocked, reviled, trampled on, tortured, slain, for acknowledging Christ; then there was strong reason for remembering His warning that to be lacking in moral courage might result in saving one's life in this world; but it might also result in losing it in the next.

Though at times the world has ceased for a while to persecute the Church, the line of her martyrs has never been broken; and the English Church has contributed its conspicuous representatives to that glorious succession. I name but two: our greatest bishop, and our greatest layman. St. Thomas of Canterbury knew for five years before his death that he would sooner or later have to lay down his life for the liberties of the Church, and with that knowledge before him, he maintained his inflexible courage, and at last deliberately returned from safety in exile to his martyrdom at Canterbury. A few hours before he suffered, being asked why he was so merry, he replied, "A man must be merry who is going to his Master." Sir Thomas More also knew, long before his martyrdom, that his fate was sealed. When called upon to bear his witness, he bore it with fortitude and joy. On the morning of his first examination at Lambeth he had confessed his sins, received absolution, and partook of the precious Body and Blood of his Divine Master, to strengthen him for the trial. As he came back to Chelsea in his boat on the Thames, there was a radiant look of joy on his face. Those who were with him asked him why he was so glad. He answered: "Because I have gone so far now, that my weakness can no longer tempt me to go back."

What lustre, too, the mission field has added to the roll of the Church's heroes! Here, where a multitude of examples might be given, one must suffice. I choose the thrilling story of the martyrdom of the three native Christian boys who, together with Bishop Hannington —himself soon to suffer death for Christ—were taken prisoner by Mwangu, King of Uganda. They were tortured, their arms were cut off, they were bound alive to a scaffolding under which a fire was kindled, and were slowly burned to death. Their enemies stood around jeering, and told them now to pray to Jesus, if they thought He could do anything to help them. The martyr spirit entered into the lads, and together they raised their voices and praised Jesus, singing until their shrivelled tongues could no longer form the sound: *Killa siku tunsifu,* an English hymn translated into the musical language of Uganda. These were the words they sang:

Daily, daily, sing to Jesus,
Sing, my soul, His praises due;
All He does deserves our praises,
And our deep devotion, too.

There is no doubt that Christians needed moral courage at the times and in the circumstances of which we
have been thinking. Are we in need of it today? Truly
the wheel of time brings strange and swift revolu-
tions. Some few years ago we would have supposed
that persecution for religious beliefs was entirely a
thing of the past. Then it would have been difficult to
imagine what we have seen come to pass in our own
day, with religious persecution begun again in many
countries of the world, where Christians have once
more been called upon to endure the confiscation of
their goods, the loss of their employment, vilification,
torture, imprisonment, and even death for their faith.
It would have been difficult to imagine that here in
England, where we still are mercifully free from official
religious persecution and proscription, the profession of
Christianity would so soon have changed from being
a social asset into being a social liability. Martyrdoms
still take place among us. They are no less real because
their scene has changed from the scaffold or the stake,
to the school, the office, the workshop, the club, wherever men and women meet together. They are no less
hard to bear because a painful death has been replaced
by a life of constant petty persecution, amid contempt
and laughter, the horrible laughter of the world, more

bitter, as has been truly said, than all the tears that men have ever shed. It is a great thing to be brave enough to die for Christ, but it sometimes requires no less moral courage to live for Him.

The reproach of the Gospel falls with heavy weight on Catholics. I have always felt that one proof of the Catholic Religion lies in the fact that it is an unpopular and persecuted Faith. Read the story of the Catholic Revival and you will find it to be one long record of martyrdom. The Tractarians were held up to the contempt and ridicule of their fellow men. Songs were written about them, they were burned in effigy, they were spat at in the streets, they were made fun of in the pantomines, they were lampooned in the Press. To take up old numbers of Punch between 1850 and 1870 is to be amazed at the vindictiveness of the attacks made week after week on the "Puseyites," as they were called. In my own experience as a parish priest I have known case after case of Catholics whose lives were made one long torment by parents, by brothers and sisters, by schoolmasters, by the people with whom they worked, because of the Faith which they professed.

What of those of us who live more sheltered lives, of whom a religious profession is expected? There is not one of us who is exempt from the temptation to moral cowardice. Our Lord did not call us to a mere outward profession of belief in Him; He called us to own His name and words by following what we know to be right, however difficult that following may be. To be ashamed of Christ and His words means to be ashamed of anything that we know to be true. A priest, let me remind myself, who panders to the prejudices or political convictions of influential members of his congregation, and preaches what he thinks will be acceptable to them instead of what he knows to be true, is as much a moral coward, with far less excuse, than one of his servers who joins in the bad talk in the factory because he is afraid of making himself disliked. Any one of us, bishop, priest, or layman, is ashamed of Christ if ever we shrink back in cowardice from avowing what we know to be right, from bearing witness to what we believe to be true, from raising our voices against what we know to be wrong. There are many of us who could honestly examine our consciences without having to confess how much we fear the world, and how often our judgment is warped and our words and actions influenced by what our friends will think about us, by a social or professional code which in our hearts we despise but have not the moral courage to ignore.

With all these things coming upon us every day, what need there is that we should pray to the Holy Ghost to stir up in us the gift of fortitude which is one of His sevenfold graces bestowed upon us at our Confirmation. Each of us should put before himself the misery that will come if the Saviour Who has redeemed us by His blood should turn away His face from us in shame because we have been ashamed of Him. We may hearten ourselves to new courage and constancy by remembering that His warning carries with it a corresponding promise. If it is true that He will be ashamed of those who are ashamed of Him, so also it is true that He will acknowledge those who acknowledge Him. He feels the shame we suffer when we brave public opinion in order to keep our consciences clear. He marks the pain and the triumph over pain, when, shrinking from putting ourselves forward, we raise our voices, face unpopularity and contempt that we may defend what we believe to be true. He is not indifferent when the tempting and easy way of falsehood lies on one side and the shame of an uncomfortable acknowledgement on the other, and, for His sake, we spurn the falsehood and choose the shame. For all of us who are willing in any way to bear the reproach of the Gospel, for us, as well as for the martyr at the stake, or the outcast for the truth's sake, stands the promise written: "Fear ye not . . . whosoever shall confess Me before men, him I will confess also before my Father which is in heaven."

Once upon a time, so runs the story, there was a king who left his palace and journeyed in disguise to a rebellious province of his dominions in order to see for himself the true cause of its disloyalty. He was a true monarch, and had about his face those princely marks, the strange divinity that doth hedge a king, so that he was quickly recognized. Captured by the insurgents, he was subjected to all manner of indignities, and finally set in the pillory while everyone pelted him with filth and used all manner of unkind words towards him. But there stood out one who rebuked them acknowledging the king for the lawful master. Him they set in the pillory side by side with his lord, and pelted him with the same filth, and loaded him with the same abuse. In course of time the king escaped, gathered his army, and subdued the rebellious province. One day, through the streets of the city where he had been so vilely used, came riding the king's troops dressed in shining armor, with plumes upon their glittering helmets. Last came the king riding in his chariot. When he came to the gates of the city, where the traitors were bound in chains, he singled out from the crowd one man who stood free and unfettered, and said to the rest, "Do you know this man? He stood with me in the day that you treated me with scorn and indignation. He shall be with me now in the day of my triumph." And amid the sounding of trumpets and the voice of acclamation, the despised and rejected citizen of that rebellious city rode through the streets side by side with his king, who set a crown of pure gold upon his head.

There is the story. Let us try to live it out, in the power and for the glory of Christ.

14

"Stunt" Religion

I CHOOSE two Bible incidents, one from each Testament, as a starting point for this chapter. The first is the story of Naaman who came to Elisha to be cured of his leprosy. He expected a dramatic and sensational cure; accustomed to the mystic incantations of the Syrian magicians, he took it for granted that the prophet would act in a similar fashion. Then came the command, "Go and wash in Jordan." Naaman was looking for the sensational and he found the commonplace. "So he turned, and went away in a rage."

For my other illustration I turn to our Lord's second temptation in the wilderness, when he resisted the suggestion to cast Himself down from a pinnacle of the temple, and to win His way to power by substituting sensation for sacrifice. What a stir it would have made if, while the courts below were thronged with worshippers, He had suddenly floated down amongst them from that dizzy height, smiling and unhurt! It would have been a spectacular fulfilment of the old prophecy that the Lord would suddenly come to His temple. Had He yielded to that impulse He would have been a nine days' wonder but not the Christ of the ages, the sensation of the world but not its Saviour.

What a tendency there is among us to despise the commonplace, and to crave for the sensational! Consider, for instance, the way we read the newspapers: we turn at once to the headlines to see if there is anything startling or dramatic—a murder mystery, a scandal in high life, a train smash or plane wreck, an earthquake, a hurricane, a riot. If we find none of these things we say, "There is nothing in the paper today." The editor knows exactly what we want and that he can increase his circulation by pandering to our morbid craving for sensationalism. That is his great temptation; if he is unscrupulous, he yields to it. Hence in newspapers of a certain type we get the "stunt," an unlovely word describing a most unlovely thing. In its proper sense "stunt" is a verb meaning to check growth or development, and this is exactly what the newspaper stunt does to the mind. Its root evil is that it deliberately magnifies the importance of some particular thing and so put it out of all perspective. That particular thing may be a political cry, or a prize fight, or a beauty contest, or a visit from a film star, or something of greater moment. Whatever the subject may be, when it is taken up as a stunt, it is given a sensational and absurd degree of importance. Things that really matter are put in the background, not merely in the newspapers, but in the minds of the public which is content to be guided by modern journalism. The craving for sensationalism is ministered to; the judgment of men becomes perverted, and they tend to lose all sense of proportion.

We see exactly the same tendency in Church life. People talk of the Church doing nothing, when actually they mean that it is doing nothing sensational. So we priests are confronted with the temptation to create excitement and stir, to make religion "popular" and salvation dramatic; to be different, eccentric and spectacular. It is a real temptation and one to be resisted at all costs. After all, it would be easy to fill a church *for a time*. My own church is an exceptionally large one, holding some fifteen hundred people, yet I could crowd it to suffocation-point for a Sunday or two if I were willing to run some thrilling stunt that would make them gape and talk. I have only to advertise in the local press that I propose to stand on my head in the pulpit on the ensuing Sunday, and there would be long lines of people waiting to get into church to see me do it. The following day there would be paragraphs in the papers with some such heading as this: "Remarkable scene in church. Priest stands on his head." The Protestant weeklies would have violent articles on new ritual excesses. My portrait would be published, or rather two portraits: one showing me the right way up, and the other standing on my head so that people might see exactly how it was done. More than that, I would only have to explain that this was Religious Eurhythmics, a new form of symbolism illustrating the theory that the world is upside down, and I should get a following. I should be bombarded with interviewers asking me to give an explanation of the latest cult, and I should receive innumerable letters from cranks who would congratulate me on my courage, and tell me that this was the new religion for which the world had been waiting. And the church, as I say, would be crowded to the doors. For what? To worship God? To listen to the message of salvation? To receive divine treasures of grace? To be healed, comforted, strengthened, sustained, uplifted, inspired?

I have purposely chosen a preposterous example because the truth is always easier to understand when we see it under a magnifying glass. My aim is grave and serious: it is to utter a protest against a tendency which I can see growing everywhere to degrade religion by making it sensational. I perceive in our churches an increasing disposition to play to the gallery, to minister to the popular love of excitement, to preach what is likely to draw at the expense of what is true, to play on the doubtful edge of heresy instead of proclaiming the Gospel of Christ crucified, to give to the people savoury tidbits on the subjects of the hour instead of solid teaching on the Faith once delivered to the saints. Nowadays anything will do that arrests attention and attracts a crowd. A Unitarian minister preaches in a cathedral pulpit; a star athlete reads the lessons in a parish church; an "open" communion is celebrated at which Protestants are invited to receive the Sacrament which is at once a Churchman's greatest privilege and the symbol and pledge of his membership in the Church; a revival meeting is held in the ballroom of a fashionable hotel, at which young men and women in evening dress bear their testimony to Christ by confessing publicly their secret sins. Indeed, some of our bishops have been affected by this tendency, so that they are tempted to think themselves failures unless by means of stunts they can continually catch the public eye and the attention of the newspapers. So, from time to time, we get sensational episcopal pronouncements which seem to be throwing over the old Faith altogether, and which cause such great pain and perplexity to the faithful. Activity of this kind does not forward the Kingdom of God. The glamour soon goes, the circus tricks quickly cease to attract, and the spangled dresses look pathetically shabby out of the limelight. It is the old commonplace and familiar Gospel of Jesus and His love that really helps the soul. It is the quiet persistent unobtrusive life of prayer and devotion, day by day, year by year, in the home, in the parish, in the diocese, that tells in the long run.

The craving for the sensational—the idea that satisfaction is to be found only in the exceptional and the spectacular—lies at the back of the longing to escape from a commonplace lot in life. It is not simply envy of those who are more fortunately placed than we are but rather the desire to do something worth doing with our lives, the feeling that we possess latent powers and slumbering capacities that are capable of so much—if only we had more thrilling and adventurous opportunities for service. We get sick to death of the prose of our living—nothing but doing the housework, or tending the children, or typing letters, or seeing clients, or catching trains, or selling goods, or preparing sermons. We cry: "O, for the wings of a dove! If only I were in a more prominent position, and had more power and more influence, I would be able to do so much more for God." We need not wait for dramatic opportunities in order to do God service. However circumscribed our surroundings, we shall nowhere find ourselves more cabined and cribbed than was the Son of God at Nazareth. Jesus lived for thirty years in very ordinary circumstances, working at a humble trade in a little village. We know from the parables exactly the kind of house He lived in as a boy. It was in a narrow street of small houses, where a man at the door could carry on a conversation with a householder in bed so that everyone in the street overheard. The home was so small that there was only one living room where the food was both cooked and eaten. There His blessed Mother must have explained to Him how leaven worked in meal, why it was useless to patch a garment beyond a certain age, and how it was that the fermenting wine burst the old skins. The marks of poverty are upon the whole. It was a house where the loss of a tiny coin meant no rest for anyone until it was found, and where as much as possible had to be made of the one lamp, by setting it where everyone could see.

It was in such commonplace surroundings that Jesus found a divine beauty and meaning that have enriched human life for ever. We may be sure that He would have found nothing drab, or humdrum, or trivial in our environment whatever it may be, or that at least He would have illuminated it so that it ceased to be monotonous and dull. We need not wait for a higher position, or for greater wealth, or for more leisure, in order to live blessed and fruitful lives. Inexhaustible treasures lie on our own doorstep. We shall find them there if we look for them, instead of wishing wistfully that we could share the romantic adventures of our favorite film or television star. Sitting by our side in the bus that takes us to work there are men and women just as interesting as the society we are so anxious to enter. To us, perhaps, they are just humanity in the mass, a collection of plodding unimaginative folk. Jesus would have woven parables about them, and there is not one of them for whom He did not die. A poet has pictured the thoughts and hopes and dreams that are pent up in one crowded bus, as the people who are travelling in it listen to a tune played on a barrel-organ:

And then the troubadour begins to thrill the golden street,
In the city as the sun sinks low;
And in all the gaudy buses there are scores of weary feet
Marking time, sweet time, with a dull mechanic beat,

And a thousand hearts are plunging to a love they'll never
    meet,
Through the meadows of the sunset, through the poppies
    and the wheat,

In the land where the dead dreams go.
There's a thief perhaps that listens with a face of frozen
    stone,
In the city as the sun sinks low;
There's a portly man of business with a balance of his own,
There's a clerk and there's a butcher of a soft reposeful tone,
And they're all of them returning to the heavens they have
    known,
They are crammed and jammed in buses, and they're each
    of them alone
In the land where the dead dreams go.

Truly, the opportunity for happy and noble living is
not far from any one of us. We go to great labor seeking after fullness of life; we journey far afield to find
it; we imagine we should achieve it if only we could
change places with someone whose life is more thrilling
and adventurous. Vain labor, vain journey, vainest of
dreams! Like the child in the fairy story we think that
the house with the golden windows lies on the other
side of the valley; but if we were to go there, we should
find, as he did, that it is our own casements that are
aglow with the westering sun. We talk a great deal
about the monotony of our lives, and yet most of it
lies in our own hearts; it is we ourselves who make the
daily path prosaic. If our hearts were but fresh, if our
spirits had in them the spring of an eternal youth, we

should find in the simple doings of every day gleaming moments which like springs in the desert would refresh our jaded souls. Fools that we are, we are always gazing out of the window to search afar for that which is waiting for us at home. As the old Hebrew proverb reminds us, "Wisdom is before him that hath understanding, but the eyes of a fool are in the ends of the earth."

The false sense of proportion which results from our love for the spectacular leads us not only to despise commonplace opportunities of service, but also to think lightly of little sins. They do not seem to be important because our standards of measurement are distorted. We fail to realize that infidelity to conscience in small things is intimately connected with a like infidelity in larger ones. Little lies are the seeds of great ones; little cruelties are the germs of serious ones; little treacheries are like holes in a piece of cloth, the beginnings of larger ones. The little sins which we commit every day, the small social falsehoods, the little acts of dishonesty in business, the trivial acts of selfishness, the passing gusts of temper, the slight habits of self-indulgence, may seem to have comparatively insignificant consequences on the outward life, but they are of incalculable influence on the interior life. They weaken the will, lower the moral tone, limit its range, destroy its sensibility, and help to put out the light of conscience. It is recorded of a lighthouse on a tropical shore that it almost failed for a most unlooked-for reason. When first kindled, the brilliant light drew about it such clouds of insects that they covered and completely darkened the glass. So it is in respect to the conscience. There is a power in it, if kept unsullied, to resist the greatest assaults, to overcome the strongest temptations; but its strength may be utterly destroyed by little venomous insect habits, each one seemingly unimportant in itself, but disastrous in collective consequences.

Take another illustration of the same truth. You can destroy a mirror by a single blow of a hammer, shivering it at once into a thousand fragments. You can also destroy it quite as effectually in a different way: go behind it with a needle and with a delicate touch make the smallest line through the silver coating at the back; the next day make a line at right angles to that; the third day make another line parallel to the first; the next, another line parallel to the second. Continue this day after day, and six months will not have passed before the mirror will be so scratched as to be worthless. Similarly, it is not necessary to commit grave and notorious sins in order to destroy the moral sense. Constant little daily faults, venial sins as we call them, if we commit them often enough, can take the silver off from the back of conscience.

It is because we think little sins are unimportant that we do not take the trouble to conquer them. We veil their danger under a false idea of their insignificance. But it is the little sins that prepare the way for the big ones. Judas began by stealing pennies, and ended by selling his Master. It is always so. There is an old Latin proverb, *emo repente turpissimus fuit*—No one ever became very bad all at once. No great sin is sudden; its genesis is to be found in the little neglected sins which have preceded it, which have gradually weakened the moral sense, and destroyed the fences that protect the soul, and made it possible for the big temptation to overcome us.

Once more, our appetite for sensationalism blinds us to many a vision of God. Why is it that God Whom we believe in, confess and worship, is so often, to put it frankly, of so little real significance to us? Why is it that He seems so dim and vague and shadowy, so far away and distant? Why is it that the thought of Him has so little influence in our lives? Is it not because we associate God with the miraculous and the spectacular, with supernatural manifestations and striking miracles of providence? We shall find God not in miracles worked on our behalf, not in audible words of divine guidance, not in sensational portents, but in simple commonplace things. Do you remember some evening when on your way back home from work you passed into a church and knelt for a few moments to say your evening prayers, and the dull and deadening mists of the world cleared away from your soul, and you found yourself gazing down a new avenue of spiritual desire? That was the voice of God. Call to mind that day when with real contrition you made your confession, and the words of absolution were spoken over you by a fellow-sinner, and a wonderful peace flooded your soul? That, too, was the voice of God. Maybe there has been a word, a sentence in this very ordinary book which has struck fire upon your spirit, and filled you with the longing for better things. That, again, is God. He speaks to us not only in church, but in the common experiences of common life. There is not a moment, there is not a place, there is not a sight, there is not a sound, in which, if we have but eyes to see and ears to hear, we may not see God's face and hear His voice. Just as in the Incarnation God revealed Himself not in a dramatic message thundered from the highest heaven, or written by a blazing finger in the sky, but in human flesh; just as in the Blessed Sacrament He uses as the veils of His perpetual presence and of the gift of Himself, not anything out of the way, not something precious or difficult to get, but bread and wine; so He manifests Himself in the simple sights and sounds of daily life. It was the sneer of the Syrians that God was the god of the hills and not of the valleys. But we live most of our lives in the valleys and seldom scale the hilltops, and it is in the valleys as well as in the hills that we may find Him:

> God of the heights where men walk free,
> Above life's lure, beyond death's sting;
> Lord of all souls that rise to Thee,
> White with supreme self-offering;
> Thou Who hast crowned the hearts that dare,
> Thou Who hast nerved the hands that do,

God of the heights, give us to share
Thy kingdom in the valleys too.

Yet through the daily, dazing toil,
The crowding tasks of hand and brain,
Keep pure our lips, Lord Christ, from soil,
Keep pure our lives from sordid gain.
Come to the level of our days,
The lowly hours of dust and din,
And in the valley-lands upraise
Thy kingdom over self and sin.

Not ours the dawn-lit heights; and yet
Up to the hills where men walk free
We lift our eyes, lest faith forget
The Light which lighted them to Thee.
God of all heroes, ours and Thine!
God of all toilers! Keep us true
Til love's eternal glory shine
In sunrise on the valleys too.

We have been treading life's common highway in
this chapter. Of all the roads that lead to Paradise I
like it best. I hope that if my readers forget all else I
have written in this book, they will at least remember
this: that I tried to show them something of the glory
of the common day, something of the honor that at-
taches to the humblest and most ordinary of duties. I
do not envy men who can show their fellowmen God's
glory in the miraculous, if only I can show them that
same glory in the commonplace. For I know that whatever else we need, we do need that—to have religion

expressed to us in the terms of common life, to find a true and living link between our commonplace experiences, and the fact of God and of His Christ. May God of His mercy grant to us one and all the gift of spiritual vision to discern the glory that is hidden in simple things, to recognize the divine Companion Who journeys with us along the common road, and to find at every halting-place a shrine.

Epilogue
"For Their Sakes"

WE READ in ancient story of a fabled city that was built to music. History, however, tells a different tale—it contains no record of any such delectable masonic labors. The only castles built to music are castles in the air, the glittering but unsubstantial fabrics of dreamland. Castles on the earth are built most often to the accompaniment of clamor and tumult, by men who hold a trowel in one hand and a sword in the other. So says the prophet Daniel when he prophesies that "the street shall be built again, and the wall, even in troublous times." He reminds us that it is not to music that we build for God, but to a din and confusion that often hide from us what we are really achieving. It is amid turmoil, difficulty, and stress that the walls of God's purpose in the world are being raised up stone on stone.

That we live in troublous times today is so obvious a

truth that it would be a waste of energy to labor it. In whatever direction we look, whether it be political, or social, or economic, the sun is obscured by dark and threatening stormclouds. Even with the surface return to religion of these recent times, it is no exaggeration to say that the Church is faced with one of the most serious crises in its history. Perhaps never, since the first ages of the Gospel, has fundamental Christian truth been denied and denounced so largely, and with such passionate animosity, as is the case in these days in most of the great nations of the world. It may well be that God has in store for His Church far greater trials to its faith and courage than any it has yet experienced. The forces that tend to disintegrate religion in English speaking countries are not yet organized by the State, as they have been in Russia, but they have already profoundly influenced public opinion, and are growing in strength. Nothing could be more childish and futile than to play a pretty game of make-believe, and pretend that all is well in Zion while the enemy is thundering at the gates. Christendom is faced with an appalling emergency, and is already fighting for its life.

However troublous the times, Christians, who believe that the victory over evil has already been won on Calvary and at the Empty Tomb, can never allow themselves to be discouraged. With the faith of the Resurrection in its heart the Church has always been at its strongest in moments of crisis, and has found in every emergency a new opportunity. So it can be today if we will prove ourselves worthy of the task to which God is calling us. "The street shall be built again, and the wall, even in these troublous times," if we rid ourselves of the defeatist spirit which is sapping our energy and destroying our morale, and cease thinking and speaking and behaving as if the battle were already lost, and Christ and His Saints were sleeping. The only true way to meet the present challenge to faith and morals is to turn from defence to attack!

If we are to do that successfully two things are urgently needed: first, a revival of apostolic zeal among us—a renewed conviction that we are put in trust with the Faith in order that we may spread it; and secondly, a resolute determination to amend our lives by God's grace, and to walk more worthy of our Christian vocation. It is my purpose in these closing pages to draw attention to the close connection between these two things, and point to the way in which they constantly react upon each other.

To begin with, a passion for souls, springing as it does from love for God expressing itself in love for man, is a most powerful motive for trying to overcome our own faults. It redeems our efforts at self-improvement from the taint of selfishness, makes us regard them as a means to an end and not as an end in themselves, and fires them with the inspiration of a great and noble cause. The true spring of Christian conduct lies "not in the hope of gaining aught, nor seeking a reward," but in the spirit of self-sacrificing service. That great word of Christ, "For their sakes I sanctify My-self," must be our watchword if we are to gain strength to rise out of the conventional standards of morality which so cramp and deaden us. The faults and failings which have been outlined in this book are so universal and so pervasive, the task of grappling with them is so continuous and so exacting, that nothing short of the highest conceivable incentive will enable us to suc-ceed in it. Such an incentive we find, and can find only, in love for God and the desire to do His will, which means, in practical effect, a longing to be fellow-workers with Him in establishing His Kingdom.

> Passionately fierce, the voice of God is pleading,
> Pleading with men to arm them for the fight.
> See how His hands majestically bleeding
> Call us to rout the armies of the night!
>
> Not to the work of sordid, selfish saving
> Of our own souls to dwell with Him on high;
> But to the soldier's splendid selfless braving,
> Eager to fight for righteousness and die.
>
> Bread of Thy Body, give me for my fighting,
> Give me to drink Thy sacred Blood for wine,
> While there are wrongs that need me for the righting,
> While there is warfare, splendid and divine.

I have tried to make this book constructive, and have suggested many remedies for the sins with which it deals. Always remembering that "without Christ we can do nothing," and that His strength is needed for our weakness, I believe that the sovereign specific for them all is to forget ourselves in the service of our fellows. It is here, I am persuaded, that the root cause of the weakness of our modern Christianity lies. It lacks the missionary spirit without which it cannot be really true to itself. It has been truly said that the Church of the majority is the Church at rest. Its chief problem is the problem of the underprivileged, of the vast number of people who are content to be ministered unto, who come to church as they would go to the theatre to take no other part in the performance than that of criticism or applause. That is why the Church makes so little progress. It is a luxury liner instead of a fishing smack, and its officers and crew have to spend most of their time in seeing that the passengers enjoy themselves, or in looking after them when they are seasick, or in preventing them from falling overboard, or in rescuing them when they do. How few there are in any congregation who carry in their souls a sense of personal responsibility for the extension of Christ's Kingdom! Outside a little handful there is the great mass of irresponsible Churchgoers who stand altogether apart from the work of evangelism, and who, even if they wish it well, never put themselves out for it, or do anything at all to help it. So they miss the inspiration to high endeavor which comes from the sense of responsibility. Once to discern our personal relation to the purpose of God for the world is to be forever purged of dilettantism; it is to be forever emancipated from the religious littleness that makes us content to be "moderately good." "For *my* sake I sanctify myself" is a *cul de sac* which will never get us anywhere. "For *their* sakes I sanctify myself" is the road that leads steadily on to perfection.

Finally, let us look at the same truth from the opposite angle, and take note of the fact that Christian living is the most powerful argument for Christianity. "Do not speak to me," Emerson once said, with a pardonable exaggeration. "What you *are* is thundering so loud that I cannot hear what you *say*." It is a simple truth, but a truth often forgotten, that we must *be* good before we can *do* good; that those who aim at God do better work for Him than those who start with the declared intention of benefiting their fellowmen. The soul that is not lighted by the hand of God and shining to His glory, may possess great intellectual abilities, it may occupy a conspicuous and influential position, it may be untiring in its energy, but it will always be an abject failure in winning other souls for God. On the other hand, there is a peculiar radiance that streams from any one, however poor and simple he may be, who is trying to follow the example of Jesus Christ. There is no mistaking it. Around really good people clings, as it were a golden mist, a transfiguring splendor which every one can perceive, though no one can analyze it; and it is this, not their intellect, nor their opportunities, nor their position, nor their activity, but their goodness which gives them their magnetic power to attract other souls to Jesus.

There is evidence on every hand that the Church has lost much of its attractive power. It is not only that the world is antagonistic—that has always been so, to a greater or less degree; it is a far more serious portent that so many of the best and most thoughtful men and women in the community are standing deliberately aloof from the Church. Many reasons are given for the neglect of Churchgoing, some of which have been suggested in an earlier chapter, but may there not be another reason altogether less flattering to our complacency? May it not be that the world can no longer see in our assemblies and in our daily conduct the abiding miracle of a God-filled and glorious Church? There is grave need among us for a revival of deep personal religion which will display itself in real sorrow of heart for the many faults and shortcomings whereby we grieve our Lord and quench His Holy Spirit; grave need of an altogether new eagerness to make sacrifices for Christ, to give ungrudgingly of our leisure and labor and means for His cause, to show by lovingkindness and unselfishness in our daily lives that we are really trying to grow into His likeness, and last, but by no means least, to endeavor by earnest and sustained devotion to improve our worship, and to learn the secret and the power of prayer.

I turn for one last illustration of my theme to the parable of the Ten Virgins in which our Lord likens the Christian character to a lamp kindled within us by the Spirit of God and meant to shine forth in such a way that men may see it and glorify our Father who is in heaven. What of our lamps? Are we keeping them supplied with the oil of grace which Christ offers us through His sacraments? Are we keeping them clean by repentance? Do we tend the wick by a life of prayer and devotion? Does the light of Christian character within us burn with as bright and clear a radiance as on the day of our first Communion? Or have we become so lax and negligent about our religion that instead of growing in grace we have fallen back, that our daily lives instead of witnessing to Jesus have become more and more conformed to the spirit of the world, and that we must confess with the foolish virgins, "Our lamps are going out"? Is the flame of Christian character burning steadily and clearly within us, or is nothing left but a dim and feeble flicker which will dwindle and expire in the first little gust of temptation or sorrow? These are solemn questions, solemn always, but surely never more solemn than today. How shall we face the Bridegroom when He comes, if, at a time when His claims are everywhere challenged and decried, we have failed to make our lives and characters a witness to His presence in the world—failed to keep our lamp shining bravely through this night of unbelief, failed "to give light to them that sit in darkness and in the shadow of death, and to guide their feet into the way of peace"?

We must arise, then, and trim our lamps, for the clock of the world is always striking midnight; and above the discordant cries of disillusionment and unbelief we can hear, if we will but listen, the voice of infinite Love calling and calling again: "Behold the Bridegroom cometh; go ye out to meet Him."